CONTENTS

3. Practice of Mission 43

Conclusion 59

PREFACE

In this day and age it is absolutely necessary for every institution to articulate as clearly as possible the purpose for its existence. The rapid changes that are bringing about complex shifts in every aspect of our societies make such constant self-definition and re-definition necessary.

The church is the Body of Christ, called into being for the purpose of participating in God's intention for the world (Jn 3.16). This Lutheran World Federation document, "MISSION IN CONTEXT: Transformation, Reconciliation, Empowerment: an LWF Contribution to the Understanding and Practice of Mission" is a contribution to the ongoing ecumenical re-articulation of what it means to be a church in our constantly changing context.

It draws from the experience of the churches, mission practitioners, students, laity and church representatives in various stations of life of the Lutheran Communion. However, it does not claim completeness, and invites every reader and every congregation to contextualize this discourse from its own perspective.

I commend it to you – to all the baptized in church and in society.

Rev. Dr Ishmael Noko
General Secretary
The Lutheran World Federation

ACKNOWLEDGEMENT

Based on a recommendation from the LWF Consultation on Churches in Mission, Nairobi, Kenya, October 1998, the LWF Council at its meeting in Bratislava, Slovakia, June 1999 gave its approval for the revision of the LWF Mission Document, Together in God's Mission: an LWF Contribution to the Understanding of Mission (Published in 1988). An Ad Hoc Team, representing LWF member churches in the seven regions, (Ethiopian Evangelical Church Mekane Yesus, United Evangelical Lutheran Church in India, the Lutheran Church in Singapore, Evangelical Church of the Lutheran Confession in Brazil, Evangelical Lutheran Church in Hungary, Evangelical Lutheran Church in Finland, Evangelical Lutheran Church in Bavaria, Germany), mission departments/societies (Church of Sweden/International Mission and Diaconia, Evangelical Lutheran Church in America/Division for Global Mission, German National Committee (AKZMD) , Finnish Evangelical Lutheran Mission) and related development agencies (Bread for the World, Germany, Canadian Lutheran World Relief) was established in 2000 to work on the revision. Five members of the Team served as a Core Group to assume responsibility for the drafting. The Team met for the first time in 2000 and, thereafter, annually until 2003 to discuss the work of the Core Group, which met more frequently. The findings of a "Mission Encounter" held in Berlin, Germany, March 2001, between theologians, mission practitioners and ecumenical partners searching for new directions in the understanding and practice of mission in the 21st Century inspired and encouraged the Core Group.

The first draft (A) was presented to the Program Committee for Mission and Development at its meeting in 2002 for discussion and comment, following which it was shared with member churches, theological institutions, mission departments/societies and related agencies to solicit further input and comments. An advanced draft (B) was shared with participants in regional pre-assembly consultations and with participants in the LWF Tenth Assembly. Further comments were received from churches and individuals and were incorporated as far as possible into the third draft (C).

Draft C was discussed by all Program Committees during the meeting of the LWF Council in Geneva, September 2004, and was approved by Council for reception with the provision that the responses and additional input received from the Program Committees be incorporated wherever possible. Three members of the Program Committee for Mission and Development, appointed to provide editorial support, approved the final draft.

It has been a long and enriching process! Many churches, agencies and individuals have participated in the making of this document: visioning, planning, writing, commenting, shaping and reshaping, editing, planning of publication, lay out, printing, distribution, etc. The whole Communion has been involved!

I should like to take this occasion to express my deep appreciation to the members of the Ad Hoc Team, the Core Group, the participants in the "Mission Encounter" for their excellent work and to all the churches, institutions, agencies and individuals who shared input and comments to strengthen the document. I should also like to express my gratitude to LWF colleagues who worked long and hard in the shaping of this document to bring it to where it is today. May we all find joy and peace in the knowledge that God will work mightily through this document for the sake of God's mission to all creation.

Rev. Dr Péri Rasolondraibe, Director
Department for Mission and Development
Editing Coordinator

INTRODUCTION

INTRODUCTION

The 1988 Lutheran World Federation mission document *Together in God's Mission: An LWF Contribution to the Understanding of Mission* expressed a holistic understanding of mission. The document also described the local church as the witness that carries God's mission across different spheres: religious, ideological, sociological, political, economic, geographic, and demographic. More specifically, the document states:

"Proclamation of the gospel, calling people to believe in Jesus Christ and to become members of the new community in Christ, participation in the work for peace and justice and in the struggle against all enslaving and dehumanizing powers are therefore an integral part of the mission of the church. All such activities point to the reality of the Reign of God and to its final realization at the fulfilment of history." (p. 9)

The theological understanding and conviction that the mission of the church, derived from its participation in God's mission, is a holistic mission, were developed further at the Eighth and Ninth LWF Assemblies in Curitiba (1990) and Hong Kong (1997). This understanding was also strongly emphasized by the Tenth Assembly in Winnipeg (2003), as stated in its message: *"Our participation in the mission of the Triune God involves the three interrelated dimensions, diakonia, proclamation and dialogue, which are integral parts of the mission of the church."* This document seeks to discuss and deepen the LWF member churches' understanding and practices of holistic mission; that is, transforming, reconciling, and empowering mission.

The LWF Consultation on Churches in Mission, held in Nairobi in 1998, underlined this holistic understanding and practice of mission as part of the Lutheran identity. The Consultation also echoed the affirmation of the 1988 LWF mission document, when it stated:

Mission encompasses proclamation, service and advocacy for justice. Mission as proclamation is an attempt by every Christian to tell and interpret the gospel story in his/her context as a way to discover God's saving action and meaningful presence in the world. Mission as service highlights the diaconal dimension of a faith active in love, working for the empowerment and liberation of those in need. Mission as advocacy for justice denotes the church's praxis in the public arena as affirmation and reaffirmation of the dignity of human life, both as individual and as community, as well as a widened sense of justice, encompassing the economic, social and ecological spheres. (Report p.20)

The Consultation envisioned transformation as an important mission imperative. This understanding of mission as transformation – of both the individual and society – deepens the empowering dimension of service as diakonia. Mission as transformation challenges the church to undergo transformation itself in order to be an instrument of transformation in the world.

Furthermore, the Consultation called for a revision of the 1988 mission document in order to better reflect and address the mission challenges and opportunities of the twenty-first century. This new document, therefore, builds on the foundation of the 1988 LWF mission document and offers a different hermeneutical approach to mission, thus strengthening the theological bases for the understanding and practice of mission for this century.

The purpose of this document is to:
• help Lutheran churches throughout the world become more deeply aware of God's mission to the world and the role of the church as the body of Christ as a part of that mission;
• serve as a tool to accompany Lutheran churches in their self-analysis and reaffirmation of mission in their respective contexts. This means inviting the church at all levels (congregational, national, regional) and related agencies to reevaluate their responsibility for mission and to stimulate them in their efforts to seek new ways of understanding their present and future participation in God's mission.

This document wishes to strengthen and deepen the church's understanding of itself as a missional church and to live it out fully. The term "missional" has been used for several years to denote mission as pertaining to the *being* of the church, while "missionary" is reserved to describe mission as the *action* of the church. For a missional church, participating in God's mission is at the core of its nature as a church.

The mission of the church is to point to and participate in the eschatological reality of the in-breaking of God's reign in the life, death, and resurrection of Jesus Christ, anticipating its final fulfillment as the basis for transformation, reconciliation, and empowerment.

A biblical model for mission

Several Bible stories provide models for the church's understanding and practice of mission. One model is suggested by the Ezekiel vision encounter (Ezekiel 37); another is Jesus' mission proclamation in Nazareth (Luke 4). No one model explains everything. Each model offers challenges and opportunities. For this document, the Emmaus road encounter (Luke 24:13–49) has been selected as the model that speaks for and enlightens a *hermeneutical spiral*

approach to mission, an approach that is reflective of the interaction between contexts, theology, and practice. It is also considered to be the best model, at this time, to convey the understanding of mission as *accompaniment*.

The mission encounter begins as Jesus walks with the disciples on the Emmaus road, sharing in their pain by listening to them as they tell their story (verse 18). Jesus then interprets the scriptures and shares with the disciples a theological understanding of God's saving act in history and reveals to them in the breaking of the bread the presence of the resurrected one in their midst. With their eyes opened to the in-breaking reign of God, the disciples, transformed by the encounter and celebrating Christ's reconciling presence, go out, empowered to share this good news with their nurturing community and others.

> *With their eyes opened to the in-breaking reign of God, the disciples, transformed by the encounter and celebrating Christ's reconciling presence, go out, empowered to share this good news with their nurturing community and others.*

Following the Emmaus road model, this document begins with a section that seeks to name and analyze the contexts of mission. The second section discusses the theology of mission, and the third section focuses on the practice of mission. Mission as transformation, reconciliation, and empowerment follows a hermeneutical spiral rather than a linear approach and is based on the dynamic view that mission is contextual. This means that the good news can only be communicated effectively to people within their own context through language and actions which are an integral part of that context. A dynamic spiral is at work when the church's understanding of its context interacts with its theology, which is intentionally incarnational (i.e., reflective of and informed by context). Such contextual theology, in turn, promotes and feeds on the praxes of mission that interact with and transform the context. Thus, the church is challenged to embark ever anew on the journey of reexamining its changing context in light of its theology and praxes, deepening the contextualization of its theology and refocusing its praxes. As in the example of the Emmaus road, the church carries out its mission as accompaniment to people in the complexity of their contexts.

CONTEXTS OF MISSION

That very day two of them were going to a village named Emmaus, about seven miles from Jerusalem, and talking with each other about all these things that had happened. While they were talking and discussing together, Jesus himself drew near and went with them. But their eyes were kept from recognizing him. And he said to them, "What is this conversation which you are holding with each other as you walk?" And they stood still, looking sad. Then one of them, named Cleopas, answered him, "Are you the only visitor to Jerusalem who does not know the things that have happened there in these days?" And he said to them "What things?" Luke 24:13–19

Section 1

CONTEXTS OF MISSION

As God's incarnation took place within a specific context (Luke 2:1–2), God's mission always takes place in particular social, economic, political, religious, and cultural contexts. Present contexts are certainly different from that of Judea 2,000 years ago, but God's reign still breaks into a specific context in today's world. Thus, engaging in mission requires prayerful discernment of the signs of the times and a faithful reading of the contexts. For an effective contextual and holistic mission, the church is challenged to engage in context discernment and analysis at local and national levels, keeping in mind the impact of global and regional factors on local contexts. This document attempts to highlight some aspects of global and regional contexts, while urging the local church to continue to deepen the process with its own contexts.

1.1. Discerning and naming the contexts of mission

The contexts in which people live shape and influence their understanding of the world, the gospel, and themselves. Therefore, the church cannot assume that its view of the world, of others, of the earth, and of God, is universal. It names its contexts to help it *be* in the world without being assimilated *by* the world (John 17), and to discern those things and people in its contexts that God seeks to transform, reconcile, and empower.

Naming a context does not consist simply in enumerating factors pertaining to the context. It involves identifying, analyzing, knowing, and categorizing in order to transform the context. It is a cooperative venture of conversation and dialogue, listening and speaking, acting and observing, giving and receiving. Interaction is an essential part of the process of naming and discovering the context of mission. Sometimes an outside voice helps the church to see its own context in a new light. More specifically, marginalized and excluded voices reveal contexts in new ways, sharpening the church's focus in mission.

In analyzing its context, the church may ask, among other things, questions relating to situations requiring transformation and/or healing, situations of conflict and reconciliation, and situations of control of power – its abuse, misuse, or the lack of it. Understanding contexts requires naming the realities and powers that are operative in the world; this includes naming both the powers of evil and the power of God. Sin, destruction, broken community and individual relationships, and ecological degradation reveal a way of life that is not as God intended. Contexts, however, are also places and situations where God is already working to bring God's promised reign to fruition. These are places where God's people are active in various callings. These are also events where the good news is proclaimed, the voices of the oppressed are heard, injustices are addressed, and creation and all people are restored to health. Mistakes may be made in the church's efforts to name its contexts. Yet without comprehending the contexts, the church may simply assume that the way things are is the way they are meant to be.

1.2. Voices that name the contexts

There are many important voices in the world which name the contexts and to which the church needs to listen carefully and intentionally. The cries of the poor, the oppressed, the excluded, and the forgotten and silenced point to the destructive arrogance of the powerful and the need for the in-breaking reign of God in Christ, where there is justice and inclusion in a life-giving community. The corrective new methods of interpretation of women's theologies, the creative voices of youth, and the testimonies of those who have experienced God's empowering presence and work in their community, enable the church to discern where in its context transformation, reconciliation, and empowerment are called for.

Understanding contexts requires naming the realities and powers that are operative in the world; this includes naming both the powers of evil and the power of God.

The scriptures, as they are shared in context, provide a different set of lenses with which to view the world and its operative values and ideals. As Jesus did when he opened the scriptures with the disciples on the road to Emmaus, the scriptures help the church evaluate its own contexts from a broader historical perspective and from the perspective of God's intentions for the world. Likewise, theological and confessional documents, with themes such as justification, grace, Word, and the sacraments, shape how the church views its contexts from a new perspective. Ecumenical engagement and the results of ecumenical and interfaith dialogue also provide a different perspective and may give new or clearer glimpses of God's reign breaking into the world, along with new possibilities and challenges for mission that may have been overlooked.

Prophets in society, within and outside the church, describe the reality of different contexts. They may

be scientists, sages, concerned women, or voices calling out in the wilderness of people's lives. They may call into question the church's assumptions and challenge it to revisit its priorities and ideals. God's creation also raises its voice to name contexts. It bears witness to the glories of God (Psalm 19:1–4), a God who delights in nourishing the physical, emotional, and spiritual life of all creation. It also painfully decries human greed and wanton violence that cause untold devastation and desolation of the environment.

There are other voices to which the church needs to listen and other analytical tools that it can use to name its context, but not all of them can be discussed here. This section describes some basic ways and tools for the church to start discerning and naming the place to which it is called to participate in God's mission and thus engage in the hermeneutical spiral.

1.3. Changing global realities affecting global and local contexts

God's mission and the resulting mission of the church take place in ever-changing contexts. The church's contexts differ from place to place and the forms of contexts may change. Nevertheless, despite constant changes and differences in contexts, there are certain overarching themes that present themselves as the church looks at the contexts of mission at the beginning of a new century. The examples given here, however, are by no means an exhaustive list of all the factors that the church needs to take into account concerning its context. In exploring its context, the church will see how issues of context affect its life and witness. It may also ask what other factors are important in shaping its context and how these factors have both positive and negative practical implications for people involved in God's mission.

1.3.1. The complex effects of globalization

The turn of the century was marked by historically significant changes, among them the fall of the Soviet Union and the end of the cold war, the rise of superpower hegemony, the dismantling of apartheid as an official justification of racism, and the information technology revolution that opened the way to globalization. Different parts of the world have become increasingly interlinked as a result of improved means of transportation and communication technologies. In general, globalization has had a considerable impact on all aspects of societal life: economy, politics, culture, communication, and the individual's sense of value and morality. On the one hand, globalization has brought a number of benefits in different aspects of life. Improved transportation allows people to travel widely with greater flexibility and efficiency and to meet people of different cultures in their own contexts. Communication technology such as the Internet has fostered the democratization of information, which can no longer be controlled or manipulated as easily by the state. Scientific and technical knowledge, best practices in different fields of human endeavor, and expectations and opportunities are shared across regional and national frontiers.

To some extent, globalization has also enhanced public scrutiny of governments, increased people's ability to respond quickly and flexibly to crises, and facilitated awareness of human rights and their abuse around the world. Socially speaking, it gives one a sense of the familiar wherever one is, and ecologically speaking, it sharpens one's sensitivity to the finiteness and interconnectedness of the ecosystem.

On the other hand, with its promotion of individualism at the expense of community, globalization has widened the gap between people, nations, and the wealthy and the impoverished. The adverse effects of neoliberal economic globalization, with its emphasis on profit making, competition, consolidation of conglomerates, and private ownership of means of production, have reduced the economy of many countries, especially in the South, to one of sheer survival. Local economies are at the mercy of transnational corporations, which dictate the course of the globalized economy. Some corporations have more wealth – and thus more power – than the majority of the world's governments. In addition to their debilitating debt burdens, impoverished nations suffer from the ill-effects of the commodification of life and bodies, the Westernization of culture, and the feminization of poverty. As a result of cash cropping, agribusiness, and severe climate change, many nations of the South are unable to maintain food security. Every year, millions of families and entire nations find themselves worse off economically. The number of educated young people without a job is on the rise.

In general, globalization has had a considerable impact on all aspects of societal life: economy, politics, culture, communication, and the individual's sense of value and morality.

Consumerism, an essential element of the neoliberal economy, comes as a challenge to the church in mission. While a high level of consumption is required to stimulate the market-based economy, the market mentality, which attributes market values to everything, including morality and religion, fuels and promotes consumerism. An economy that thrives on spending more rather than saving is detrimental to the sustainability of the earth's resources for future generations. Advertising has encouraged consumerism even in places where poverty predominates.

It often blurs the distinction between wants and needs and its emphasis on purchasing rather than recycling has a detrimental effect on society and the environment.

The church in mission is challenged to address economic injustices and to question any view that defines or evaluates people according to their wealth or market value (cf. LWF Working Paper, *"Engaging Economic Globalization as a Communion,"* May 2001).

As the globalized consumer economy continues, the devastation of the ecosystem intensifies. As rainforests continue to be destroyed and the use of pesticides has increased to maximize profits, the amount of land suitable for growing crops has decreased due to growing desertification. The trend toward corporate farming has generated unemployment and consequent migration from the countryside to the cities, highlighting the connection between ecological and economic issues. Encroachment of certain predatory aspects of Western civilization to other areas of the earth, rapid world population growth, and harmful cultural traditions have led to the extinction of many species of animals and plants and threaten the delicate balance of fragile ecosystems.

Technological advances and modern conveniences have often come at the expense of land, air, and water. Pollution by chemicals, noxious emissions, and radiation threatens the well-being of all creation. God's creation has suffered greatly at the hands of sinful human beings. Yet, at the same time, technological advances have allowed people to discover, trace, and eliminate other harmful practices and substances. For example, pharmacological advances and the discovery of radiation's role in diagnosing illness have saved countless lives throughout the world.

1.3.2. Technological contexts

Along with globalization has come an increased use of technology and greater access to information. Information technology has both positive and negative aspects. On the positive side, people can communicate with each other more freely and immediately, and the ability to store, retrieve, process, and disseminate information has increased. People are

© CAM Barbara Robra

also able to transcend the traditional geographical boundaries of religions. Information technology may also allow the church to reach out to people who have withdrawn from institutional religious communities.

On the negative side, "virtual" contact may become more important than personal contact. Moreover, information technology runs the risk of increasing the gap between those who have access to this technology and those who do not. The wealthy have easier access to technological innovations than the poor, driving a greater wedge between the affluent and poor nations and individuals of the world.

There is a flourishing global market in the genetic engineering of animal and plant life. Genetically modified food is creating new dependencies, even though the physiological consequences are not yet known. The genetic patenting of indigenous plants by global agricultural corporations develops and supports the ongoing process of dependency and deprivation of the right to ownership of Southern countries.

While globalized women's movements have opened doors for many women in terms of affirming their rights over their own bodies, the globalization of economics and entertainment media has increased the exploitation of women as surrogate mothers and has reduced women's bodies to objectivized commodities or ovum donors. The possibility of knowing a child's sex before birth has led to an increase in abortions of female fetuses in places where male children are considered more desirable.

The ability to do something does not necessarily mean it is right. Scientists exercise significant power in a world that idolizes technology, and there is a temptation to abuse this power for military and other aims. As it engages in mission and gains a glimpse of God's in-breaking reign in Christ, the church encounters ethical dilemmas about the value and use of technologies. It has to take seriously into account what is appropriate and keep in mind cultural integrity and public accountability.

1.3.3. Health contexts

Advances in scientific knowledge and technology have led to considerable progress in combating various diseases and other threats to health. Nevertheless, despite technological progress, the world continues to struggle with health issues. The intensity of that struggle, however, differs from one continent to another. Even in the twenty-first century, the connection between illness and poverty is striking. In many countries in the South, and also in pockets of poverty in affluent countries, the poor are more prone than the rich to ill-health. Illness weakens the frail economies of the countries of the South.

> *The genetic patenting of indigenous plants by global agricultural corporations develops and supports the ongoing process of dependency and deprivation of the right to ownership of Southern countries.*

Today's world is marked by different physical, mental, psychological, emotional, spiritual, and relational and social illnesses, some of which are acknowledged, while others are kept hidden and are the object of denial. Among the latter are killer diseases such as HIV/AIDS, tuberculosis, and malaria, which devastate entire continents. HIV/AIDS has reached pandemic proportions in many countries of the South. Economic, cultural, and other factors have affected the ability of some countries to react appropriately. Although primarily a health issue, it also creates serious social and economic problems, among them an increasing number of orphans and the inability of families affected by AIDS to provide for themselves. In some places, children and women are becoming much more vulnerable and burdened. Educational health programs are important, as is the need to break the silence about this illness and other health issues. The church has had trouble talking about this issue publicly, yet this crisis constitutes a challenging opportunity for the church in mission.

Illness may result in permanent impairment. Disabling conditions, however, are not illnesses. Approximately 10 percent of the population in any given country have one of the five broad categories of disability: physical disability, blindness, deafness, intellectual impairment, and mental illness.

Such people face discrimination when seeking employment and at their place of work. Public buildings, work places, and even churches are not always accessible to people with ambulatory problems. Increasingly, churches are making efforts to provide ways for people with disabilities to participate fully in church life and work (e.g., sign language interpretation for the deaf). Working with others in educating society to remove physical obstacles and cease the stigmatization and exclusion of people with disabling conditions is an urgent challenge for the church.

1.3.4. Violence in the world

God's mission has always taken place in the midst of a violent world. The crucifixion was an act of violence against God and, indirectly, against humanity and all creation. The mission of the church began in the midst of persecution and violence. Violence, in all its forms, overt or covert, has always been used to gain power over others. It is a potent tool used by those with power or seeking power to control, suppress, or enforce change for their own benefit. It is a sin.

War and conflict: Violence, conflict, and war occur between or within nations as power struggles to maintain or increase control over limited resources and achieve uncontested superiority. In the past, conventional wars may have been fought by the military with predetermined rules of engagement. More recently, insurrectionists, rebels, and warlords have engaged in armed conflict. Innocent civilians, especially children and women, are dragged into these conflicts and used as pawns, shields, and targets. The use of terror as a forceful means to break the enemy has always accompanied armed conflict. Today's technological advances make this form of violence even more lethal, physically and psychologically.

War brings untold suffering, disease, and poverty to the most vulnerable, the elderly, women and children, and to succeeding generations. It devastates infrastructures and the environment.

Equally destructive is the covert violence of geopolitical and economic warfare on impoverished nations. This occurs when aid is contingent upon adopting various policies that benefit the giver at the expense of the recipient. The illegitimate debts of countries in the South, and the facilitation of investment across borders to maximize profit to the detriment of those countries where investments are made, are examples of covert violence. Poverty itself is a form of violence, for it robs people of their human dignity, health, and well-being.

Structural and systemic violence: Violence occurs when social structures are founded on and maintained by privileged groups for their own benefit. Patriarchal structures, for instance, do not recognize the rights and equality of women. Migrant groups are exploited and immigrants treated unjustly for ethnic, racial, sexual, or religious reasons. Social stratification is another form of social violence. The "untouchables," or those with the lowest social standing in society, are often unjustly excluded. Social or political structures such as dictatorship, oligarchy, and patriarchy have always resulted in systemic violence. It foments the suppression of human and civil rights, the implementation of unjust political policies, and the unilateral imposition of regional values, ideologies, and economics. Gender, race, ethnicity, religion, sexual orientation, and even language have been used as the basis on which people have been excluded or rendered voiceless. In extreme cases, this can lead to so-called ethnic cleansing and genocide. Throughout history, systemic violence has not gone unchallenged. Counter-violence, including the use of terror at national and regional levels, has caused protracted suffering and destruction.

Violence against women, children, and the weak: Violence is also the cause of terrible suffering in the home, often directed against women, children, the elderly, and

© CAM Barbara Robra

the disabled. Such people can be abused physically, sexually, and mentally. Battered women are isolated from nurturing, supportive communities in order to exercise greater control over them. Violence may also take the form of inequity in salaries and opportunities between men and women, and "glass ceilings" in the corporate sector. Exclusive language renders silent and nameless half of the world's population (cf. LWF document *Churches say "NO" to violence against women*, 2001). Children may be malnourished or denied education. Violence includes forcing children to fight in wars and into prostitution and child labor.

Violence against the elderly and the ageing occurs when institutions destroy their dignity or sedate

© LWF

them heavily, or when their own children and society abuse them financially, socially, physically, or intellectually. The wisdom of the elderly is often rejected or suppressed, their contributions in transferring values and experiences of life to new generations forgotten. The church in mission is called to address this violence in ways that encourage community rather than isolation from community.

Violence in religion and in the church: Religious fanaticism is a sad fact of human history. It breeds violence that may be directed inward in attempts to purify and cleanse the church or religious body, or outward, against people of other religions or even other denominations. In one sense, this is violence in its worst form, for it justifies itself in the name of religion and in the name of God. This violence has been practiced overtly by fanatical zealots in all religions, and covertly through misinformed views and understandings of other religions, which directly influence the understanding of mission.

> *Gender, race, ethnicity, religion, sexual orientation, and even language have been used as the basis on which people have been excluded or rendered voiceless.*

The church is not always the victim of violence, though that is often the case. The church has also been violent towards its own members. Colonial churches exercised power over developing mission churches, often preventing the younger churches from forming their own leadership and sense of mission. Abuse of power and disputes over property by church authorities have often been the cause of church conflicts. Women have been subtly and obviously excluded from leadership and oversight positions in the church, and their voices, as well as those of youth, have been silenced or ignored.

Violence seeks to isolate and separate people from their communities and from their sources of nurture and hope. It treats people as less than human. Violence is a sin that attempts to suppress and negate all signs of hope and community in God. The church in mission is called to name and shame this violence and walk with those who seek justice and peace for their empowerment.

1.3.5. Religious, cultural, and political contexts

In many parts of the world, in spite or because of violence and calamity, there is a surge in spirituality: people are seeking new forms of spirituality to satisfy their longing to belong. Often, the institutional church does not seem to offer the spiritual satisfaction they seek. In many countries in Europe – described by analysts as post-Christian, postmodern, highly secularized, and market driven – churches have experienced extensive loss of membership due to a general lack of interest in church life and mission. What had been referred to as Christendom is no more. New or rediscovered forms of religion are instead taking advantage of the search for spirituality. Some have left institutional religions to develop rediscovered cultural roots, to engage in spiritism, or to embrace secularization.

A new challenge for the church in mission, especially in the North, is to address the religious and cultural plurality in its midst. Large-scale migration of people across regions and continents, seeking financial opportunities or fleeing from oppression and violence, has led to an ever-larger diversity of religion and cultures in the major cities of the world. Religious cultures are no longer isolated from each other. In such multicultural situations people feel that their self-understanding or identity is brought into question. They seek their roots and a meaning or purpose in life. Many are involved in constant processes of self-construction or "identity projects." This is evident in youth culture and among migrants, but it is also a feature of most people's lives. Identity projects happen at both the individual and collective level, when people endeavor to shape or reshape their individual or collective identity, or even try to rewrite history. This perspective may help explain the causes of regional conflict, and may also shed light on the increase of fundamentalism and nationalism. Churches in host countries to immigrants or refugees are challenged to engage in daily interaction through dialogue and hospitality.

One response to increasing religious plurality has been a reactionary fundamentalism, with its strong desire for groups to protect themselves and their

identity from outside influences or to recover a passionate loyalty to an idealized traditional religious belief. The need to recover or emphasize the fundamentals of one's faith is important and empowering to the self, as the inherent dynamics of fundamentals have a transforming influence on the individual, the religious community, and the wider society. Fundamentalism, however, makes absolutes of such fundamentals and imposes them upon everyone in the community. When it is connected with political and economic power, reactionary fundamentalism can be used to justify opposition or violence to outsiders.

A comprehensive cultural shift, described as the transition from the modern to the late or postmodern society, has been identified as one of the most challenging contexts of mission. This cultural shift is closely associated with globalization and considered as its social, cultural, and religious repercussions. It is characterized by a radical questioning of received conceptual schemes and what was previously held as truth and authority. Nothing can be taken for granted in science, religion, or the search for stability in family patterns or traditional forms of authority. In a world where the meaning of language and hermeneutics is

given prominence in the scientific community, the feeling of insecurity will rise. When theological truth is questioned, the mission of the church in the world is challenged. By means of global processes of influence these phenomena, arising in the North, do not remain there, but are already felt in different parts of the world.

Christians live and work in different political contexts. There are differences of opinion over whether governments participate in or oppose the mission of God. People may confuse the reign of God with political power, especially when the term "Kingdom of God" is used. Good governance makes it tempting to assume that it is "blessed by God" and that such a system is ordained for all cultures. Every system of governing, however, imposes its contextual and ideological perspectives upon society. The imposition of political ideologies may silence the voices of people, rob them of their dignity, foster systemic violence, or lead to global conflict. Bad governance may hinder access to adequate educational, health, security, or organizational resources. Yet God's mission takes place in the midst of the ambiguities of these contexts.

> *A comprehensive cultural shift, described as the transition from the modern to the late or postmodern society, has been identified as one of the most challenging contexts of mission*

1.4. Context and theology

Some of the realities of present day contexts, which have implications for the church's mission and theology, have been named. The disciples on the Emmaus road saw their context differently when Jesus opened up the scriptures and revealed himself to them as the resurrected Christ in the breaking of the bread. This enlightenment was necessary for them to make sense of and to address their context in a way that would help and empower them for mission. The church, too, needs to reflect critically on its theology and practice of mission in the light of the Word of God made alive by the Holy Spirit within each context.

Context and theology relate to each other in a dialectical and dialogical manner aptly described as a *hermeneutical spiral*. Theology traces its origin in the hearing of the Word of God in context, followed by faith commitment. The "faith active in love," born of the hearing and working of God's creative Word, expresses itself in praxis; that is, an activity that seeks to incarnate the gospel in the life and context of a community. Christian theology is a faithful reflection on God's being and acting in the world and on the praxis of the church and the individual. Theology of mission, more specifically, reflects on God's mission and on the church's response to Christ's gracious call to follow him.

As it reflects on praxis, Christian theology is necessarily contextual: while it addresses the context, it is influenced and to a deeper extent conditioned by the context. Theology, therefore, needs to be challenged continuously and transformed by the Word of God from scriptures. The disciples on the Emmaus road had their acquired theology about the Christ challenged and transformed by the risen Christ. A theology that is capable of articulating God's mission must be transformed continually by the Word heard in context and in praxis.

Moreover, theology, drawing from a long history and wealth of Christian tradition and confessions, sharpens the church's analysis and naming of the context. Serving the missional church faithfully in the dialectical tension between praxis in context and the creative word of God, theology enables the church to think clearly about its engagements in the world and strengthens the church's understanding of its reason for being.

THEOLOGY OF MISSION

And he said to them, "O foolish men, and slow of heart to believe all that the prophets have spoken! Was it not necessary that the Christ should suffer these things and enter into his glory?" And beginning with Moses and all the prophets, he interpreted to them in all the scriptures the things concerning himself. Luke 24:25–27

THEOLOGY OF MISSION

© CAM Barbara Robra

2.0. Introduction

The theme of God's people being sent into the world to herald the breaking in of God's gracious reign in Christ appears throughout the New Testament, although the word "mission" is not found in the scriptures. From the sixteenth century, due to historical circumstances, mission became attached to conquest, colonialism, cultural and religious imperialism, and the implantation of Western Christianity across the globe. Today, there are different connotations to the word "mission," and there is confusion and even aversion to the term. It is hoped that discussing the theological grounding of mission, using the hermeneutical spiral approach, will provide some clarity about the different understandings of mission and retrieve it from past abuse.

The Word of God in the scriptures, brought to life in context by the working of the Holy Spirit, is the foundation of the church's faith, life, mission, and theology. Although the different parts of scripture do not appear to be uniform, the Lutheran tradition holds to the view that scripture interprets and explains itself, disclosing what is essential and

What is scripturally essential is the good news that Jesus the Christ is the Savior and foundation of the faith, and the source of all transforming missions.

what is not. What is scripturally essential is the good news that Jesus the Christ is the Savior and foundation of the faith, and the source of all transforming missions. The Word awakens faith, by means of which it unites a person with the living God, thus opening a new reality in Christ, who is present in faith through the Holy Spirit. It is the same Holy Spirit that sustains faith, empowering it to be faithful to the Word and free for mission (John 14:12; Romans 6:22, 7:4).

The mission of the church will continue until the fulfillment of God's reign. According to the witnesses of scripture, God's reign is eschatological; that is, a reality of end time which is already coming, breaking into lives and contexts in the here and now. In Jesus the Christ, the fullness of God has been revealed (Colossians 1:19, 2:9). With this revelation, God's new heaven and earth (Revelation 21) is breaking into the existing world. The present creation *already* participates in the new creation. A decisive sign of God's reign is the overcoming of death on the cross by Christ's resurrection, which opened up a new future for humanity with God.

The world and human beings, however, as part of the old creation, are still under the sign of the cross and not yet fully redeemed. Sin's destructive power,

though already conquered on the cross, still affects people's way of life in the world. Sin has destroyed harmony in the created world and brought to the world alienation, guilt, and shame. It has caused the estrangement of human being from God, the self, neighbors, and nature. This "already and not yet," as the apostle Paul describes it, is the basic tension of Christians' faith, speaking, and daily living and is constitutive of the church's mission contexts.

The missiological perspective on God's reign calls for further discussion among the churches. More clarity is needed on the difference between the reign of God as God's presence in the world since creation and the in-breaking reign of God in Christ. Likewise, clarity is needed on the difference between the reign of God and the traditional concept of the "Kingdom of God" with the possibility for one to be outside the Kingdom, by one's own choice, and the in-breaking reign of God in Christ. The choice for "reign of God" instead of "Kingdom of God" is not based simply on a preference for inclusive language. The in-breaking reign of God in Christ affirms God's reign in creation, on account of the Incarnation, but it is, at the same time, the confirmation of its final consummation, ushered in by Christ's resurrection. Moreover, God's eschatological reign in Christ expresses in a dynamic way God's interaction with and action in the world. Comparatively, the term "Kingdom of God" is very static and space bound, and thus could be easily confused with the concept of Christendom.

> *A decisive sign of God's reign is the overcoming of death on the cross by Christ's resurrection, which opened up a new future for humanity with God.*

2.1. The mission of God

Throughout the ambiguities of life and the tribulations of a violent world, the church has learned to trust in the revelation of scriptures that the God of Jesus Christ is a God who is present and acts in love in and for the world. God is in mission. In Jesus, God has come to the "far away country"; God lived and died together with the lost son in order to bring him home, with all the dignity of God's children (Luke 15:11–24). The mission of the one loving God is a mission of mercy and grace and not of desert and might. God's grace, overcoming the consequences of sin – alienation, death, and depravity – extends beyond the individual to all communities, to all creation. All God's creation has been touched by this grace and is therefore awaiting transformation (Romans 8:22–23).

This God in mission, who creates and sustains the universe and yet becomes vulnerable in and at the hands of God's own creation, is a Triune God. Trinity describes "God in mission" as always a God for others; namely, the whole of humankind, the world, the entire creation. The Trinity is a communion in mission, empowering and accompanying the One who is sent, the beloved, to impact the world with transformation, reconciliation, and empowerment. For the ongoing mission of God, the Father and the Spirit send the Son, the Father and the Son breath in the Spirit, and the Son and the Spirit reveal the glory of the Father to the far reaches of the universe. This sending, yet accompanying and empowering, of the beloved, this reaching out for others, and thus the acceptance of vulnerability in love, is characteristic of the Trinity. It is this love that unites the Triune God.

> *The Trinity is a communion in mission, empowering and accompanying the One who is sent, the beloved, to impact the world with transformation, reconciliation, and empowerment.*

2.1.1. God's mission as Creator

The biblical view of God's mission in creation affirms a relationship between God and the world. God created the world from nothing out of God's gracious will. Thus, the world is totally dependent on God who, as the source of all life, sustains, replenishes, transforms, and renews life in the world (Psalm 104). Creation belongs to the heart and substance of the gospel, for God's limitless love and goodness are manifested in creation.

In love, God has also shared God's mission in creation with all people, created in God's own image to be God's co-workers. Women and men, as God's stewards, are accountable to God for the care of creation. This responsibility of the "created co-creator" is intricately connected with human dignity. God in grace also sustains the world by working within human institutions and societies. It is the vocation of those who confess God's name to work in partnership with all people for the realization of God's purpose of peace and wholeness. This includes work for justice, trust among peoples, freedom from hunger, responsible use of the earth's resources, and the proper use of technology for human welfare.

Although humankind and the whole creation suffer from the powers and consequences of sin (Romans 8), as the context painfully attests, these do not have the final word. The message and reality of creation include also the promise that God will "make all things new" (Revelation 21:5). The Trinitarian God, therefore, is calling people to participate in mission in creation, which even now, in the midst of evil, anticipates the coming consummation. Transformation and justice, forgiveness and reconciliation, healing and empowerment, are the signs of the future of the world with God. Christians, in their own contexts, can strengthen these encouraging signs in many ways.

2.1.2. God's mission as Redeemer

Jesus' life, work, suffering, death, and resurrection reveal God's unconditional love for the world God created (John 3:16). The wholeness of mission requires that all essential Christological aspects be taken into consideration. The life, teaching, and ministry of Jesus set an example to the Christian as to how mission should be done: Jesus' personal "manifesto" in the synagogue of Nazareth (Luke 4:16–20); the sending of the disciples (Matthew 10); Jesus' teaching and parables; his healing and feeding of the hungry; the status, dignity, and importance he gave to women and to their participation in his ministry. More importantly, however, God's mission as redeemer is revealed in *the way of the Son*, namely, the way of incarnation, the way of the cross, and the way of resurrection.

Incarnation offers a model for holistic mission, because, through incarnation, God enters into the totality of human existence. The birth of Jesus means the realization of the most central promise in God's mission: the sending of the Son into the world to save it. In Jesus, God became human in a particular place, time, and culture. He subjected himself to human conditions. He identified himself with people, entering into solidarity with anyone in need. In Jesus, God disclosed the original intention of creation and true humanity. *The way of incarnation* is a way of transformation and reconciliation.

The way of the cross is God's powerful way of saying *no* to sin and injustice and standing for love and justice in spite of persecution and crucifixion.

© CAM Barbara Robra

injustice and oppression. In reality, in the depths of every oppression and exclusion, as experienced in context, is the crucified God. However, Christ's crucifixion neither sanctifies unjust suffering nor provides a model for how suffering should be borne. Rather, it is a witness to God's desire that no one should suffer violence. *The way of the cross* is a way of reconciliation and empowerment.

Christ's *resurrection* is the single event that has deeply transformed the world. Violence, death, and the terror that its finality brings no longer have the last word. Resurrection opened a new reality of liberation and hope for humankind and the whole creation. God is reconciled with humankind and creation through Christ's death and resurrection. God also opened up reconciliation between human beings and between humankind and creation. Moreover, Christ's resurrection reveals the true nature of things. Creation itself takes on a new dimension. Every created thing, every moment and event, is pregnant with life-giving potentialities; nothing is allowed to have finality, even would-be "dead ends" are transformed into opportunities for mission. *The way of resurrection* is a way of transformation and empowerment.

2.1.3. God's mission as Sanctifier

God's mission continues in the world through the Holy Spirit. The Spirit of God empowered the prophets, descended on Jesus from the beginning of his ministry, indwelled and empowered the first disciples, and sent and equipped the nascent church for its witness. In the same way, the Holy Spirit calls, sends, and enables all of God's people in every age, irrespective of gender and age, for participation in mission.

Through the gospel, the Holy Spirit calls people to repentance, faith, and new life. It is the Spirit who gathers into one body a new family, a diversity of

In identifying himself with the suffering of people and bearing their sins on the cross, Jesus Christ penetrated into the deepest darkness of human existence and overcame the power of death. Christ's death effects salvation, which concerns the whole world: "God was in Christ reconciling the world to himself" (2 Corinthians 5:19). The cross of Christ also reveals God's way of solidarity with the excluded and oppressed, as well as a way of protest against

The way of incarnation is a way of transformation and reconciliation. The way of the cross is a way of reconciliation and empowerment. The way of resurrection is a way of transformation and empowerment.

human beings, breaking the barriers of class, race, gender, and culture. It is not the messengers but the Holy Spirit who convicts of sin and injustice, who arouses faith, and who renews God's people for mission, individually and collectively. In the power of the Holy Spirit, the proclaimed Word reaches out and seeks to transform even those who are far from the reign of God – those who oppose, ignore, or distort the gospel.

The lasting fruits of mission are the work of the Holy Spirit. The Spirit enables imperfect human efforts to become instruments of God's mission. The Holy Spirit transforms human words proclaiming the Good News, the water of baptism, and the bread and wine of the Eucharist into signs of Christ's presence in the church, empowering the church for God's mission. The Holy Spirit equips Christians and the whole church with a diversity of gifts (1 Corinthians 12; Romans 12; Ephesians 4). Equipped with these spiritual gifts (*charismata*), they are able to proclaim the gospel and share the life described by the gospel with all peoples in every place. All of the Spirit's gifts – preaching, teaching, healing, prophecy, administration, and others given to women and men – are intended to strengthen the communities of God's gathered people, congregations, for inner growth and holistic mission. The Spirit makes the church, imperfect though it is, a foretaste of the promised age to come.

2.2. The church in mission

The Trinity, as a "community of divine sending," has created a space for the church to take part in God's mission, to be sent, empowered, and accompanied by grace into the "end of the earth." Receiving the church, with all its human frailty, into the divine missional communion (1 Corinthians 1:9) shows the depth of God's love and the extent of God's vulnerability. The church in mission refers to the local assembly of believers empowered by God's Word and Sacraments and led by the Holy Spirit to participate in God's mission. This church extends in space to include different levels of fellowship and communion and different expressions. It also extends in time to include preceding and succeeding generations. The church in mission is the Body of Christ in the world.

The church's participation in God's mission, therefore, is a gift of God's grace, a gift grounded in and flowing from the in-breaking reign of God in Christ. Created out of grace to be part of the divine communion, the church does not live for its own self, but for God and for the world. "Predestined to be conformed to the image of God's Son" (Romans 8:29), the church does not only participate in the fulfillment of God's mission, but is also at the same time the sign of its presence.

Thus, the mission of the church is of the gospel, not of the law, for God's redeeming grace has set the church free from a compulsive pursuit of success and results for its own sake. The success of mission cannot be measured principally with human expectations and reasoning. As the church follows its Lord faithfully, trusting in the presence of the resurrected Christ in its life and witness, its mission also reflects

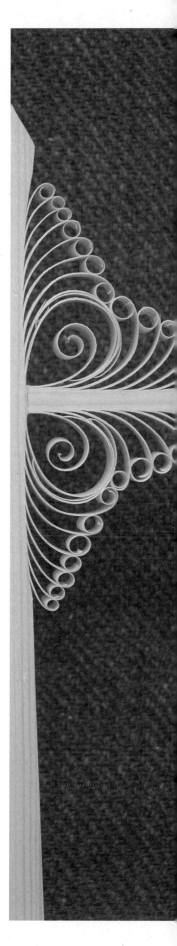

the vulnerability of unconditional love shown on the cross of Christ. In God's mission human defeat often turns to victory, for Christ's power is made perfect in weakness (2 Corinthians 12:9).

2.2.1. Mission is of the being of the church

The reason for being of the church, as Jesus indicates, is to participate in God's mission: "As the Father has sent me, I am sending you" (John 20:21). The church is God's own people created to declare the wonderful deeds of the One who called them out of darkness into God's marvelous light (1 Peter 2:9). Thus, mission is of the very being of the church. To be in mission is not optional for the church. Mission is constitutive of its being as the "one, holy, catholic, and apostolic" church (Nicene Creed).

Mission and the one, holy, catholic, and apostolic church

The church as the Body of Christ is one and it participates in the one mission of the Triune God. Due to human weakness, the church has not yet realized the oneness it confesses to be, but has tried over the centuries to approximate it by endeavoring to engage in mission in "unity in diversity." Christians have always confessed that the disunity of the church is detrimental to its witness to the love of God. Christ's high priestly prayer that "they all may be one … that the world may believe" (John 17:21) has also become a prayer of the church as it longs for the day when it will be the one "Body of Christ." The unity of the church is one of the purposes of mission. For the different churches, participating together in God's mission in ecumenical joint ventures is a way to experience unity, thus strengthening their effort in ecumenical dialogues.

The church is *holy* because it is a communion that God loves and sanctifies by setting it apart for mission. The church's holiness, therefore, is not in its "otherness" vis-à-vis the world, but is expressed precisely in its being in the world, participating in God's mission through its being, presence, and acts in a violent and wounded world. As the church points to the grace and love of the holy One in the midst of the self-destroying world, there is a deep sense of longing for and expectation of holiness. The church in its mission points to the sacredness of life and of all God's creation. In its presence it witnesses, even without words, to the dignity and sanctity of sustained creation.

The church in mission is *apostolic* in that it is empowered, sent, and accompanied into mission by the "divine community of sending," namely the Triune God. The apostolicity of the church has to do primarily with being sent with a message of good news to the world (Matthew 28:18–20). It thus points to the crucial role of the ministry of Word and Sacraments in strengthening the church for mission.

Whether or not inviting people to the grace of baptism is an integral part of the apostolicity of the church has been much debated in some parts of the Lutheran Communion. Some church leaders in Asia, for instance, argue it is theologically sound to hold that unbaptized believers belong to the one, holy, catholic, and apostolic church by virtue of their faith. Therefore, they consider it unnecessary to expose these believers to the social, political, and economic hardship associated with being baptized, a situation that is prevalent in their part of the world. Lutheran churches in other contexts, however, firmly believe that "baptizing people in the name of the Father and the Son and the Holy Spirit" is part of the apostolic mandate of the church.

Moreover, apostolicity refers less to church hierarchy and authorities than to the apostolic faith active in mission through women and men. Apostolicity highlights the fundamental nature of the church as being sent. Apostolicity also denotes that the One who sends is always present and active through the incarnational mission of the church. Sending, however, does not necessarily imply going to far away countries or cultures, even though cross-cultural witnessing is an essential part of sending. In today's globalized world, the ends of the earth are often close to home.

© LWF Margret Stasius

Mission and the catholicity of the church

The catholicity of the church, understood from the perspective of mission, refers generally to the geographic spread of the Christian faith throughout the world and the presence of the church in every locality among countless cultures and subcultures. The Christian faith, like leaven, not only permeates the whole dough, but also transforms it. The emphasis, however, is more on the qualitative universality of faith and its incarnational implantation into every culture, rather than on the quantitative spread of the church. This qualitative universality encompasses believers of all times – God's people of past generations, of today, and of years to come. The catholicity of the church is also a reminder that all of God's creation will eventually be united and renewed in Christ.

The Christian faith, for all its universality, is also culturally bound. Faith is by nature incarnational, firmly committed to a time, a place, and a culture. As local congregations endeavor to engage in mission, they must seek a balance between locality and universality, for universality and particularity are inseparably connected with each other. Without the universal communion of faith, each local church is unable to find a genuine self-understanding in

> *Thus, mission is of the very being of the church. To be in mission is not optional for the church. Mission is constitutive of its being as the "one, holy, catholic, and apostolic" church.*

© CAM Barbara Robra

not a strategic association or alliance for practical purposes that can be abandoned if proven not to be beneficial. It is a reality reflecting the identity of the church as one sharing in God's very being.

Used ecclesiologically, the term "communion" expresses three levels of church relations: first, the unity of the church across all times and space; second, the nature of life together in the local church; third, the relationship between local churches in a regional and global context. Understanding the church as communion has direct implications for the understanding and practice of mission. Engaging in mission as communion brings a qualitative difference to mission. Since the mission of the church is not for its own glorification, churches of the same tradition in different regions and of different traditions in the same region can join their efforts, ecumenically, in a common mission venture. Communion that maintains the spirit of unity and catholicity expresses itself in humble commitment, respect for one another, forbearance, patience, and love. The tendency to compete for mission fields in different parts of the world, in the race to expand the profile and sphere of influence of one's own denomination or organization, should be replaced by cooperation and joint action. Competition and the idea of "conquest," as well as proselytism (attracting other Christians to one's own denomination), jeopardize and undermine God's mission.

the local context. For the church in mission, therefore, catholicity or universality without contextuality leads to imperialism, and contextuality without catholicity leads to provincialism.

Mission and the church as communion and ecumenical fellowship

The reality of the communion of churches is rooted in the communion of the Triune God through Christ (1 Corinthians 1:9). Communion, therefore, is

Sharing in joint/ecumenical mission ventures in different parts of the world strengthens the communion of churches. Partnership in mission expressed in commitment with one another and in the sharing of mission resources – be they spiritual, human, material, or financial – removes any sense of superiority, isolation, opportunism, and suspicion. Churches that do mission together are apt to maintain the spirit of unity, mutuality, learning, and sharing from one another and to experience the blessing of life in communion.

The vision and practice of communion can help the church address the prevalent fragmentation and division of communities and bring healing to a world broken by greed and violence. As members one of another (Romans 12:5), church members are called "to build up each other" (1 Thessalonians 5:11) and "love one another with mutual affection" (Romans 12:10). Thus, the church as communion can invite communities to share responsibility and promote a just society.

2.2.2. Mission is Word empowered and Spirit led

The church is the creation of God's dynamic Word (*creatura verbi*). It is sustained, inspired, and empowered by the Word for mission. God's Word sustains the life of faith through the ambiguities and temptations of the ever-changing contexts of the church. It also equips God's people for every good work (2 Timothy 3:16) and thus enables it to address the needs of specific contexts. The Word creates in the church both the will and the insights to participate in God's in-breaking reign.

The Sacraments as "visible Word" are also related inseparably to mission and its goals and praxes. In baptism, the Christian church has found the promise of unconditional grace, forgiveness, and a new life in Christ: a life of discipleship. Baptismal grace nurtures this life of discipleship throughout a Christian's lifelong journey of "faith active in love." In baptism, believers are called to communion with the Trinity in mission and, by the same calling, are sent and accompanied by the Holy Spirit into the world with a message of love. Baptism is a commissioning for mission in which each member of the church has his or her own vocation and task.

Mission spirituality can also be found in the Eucharist, in which Christ himself is present with the church in and with the bread and wine, giving his body and blood for the forgiveness of sins, sharing his life with the world. As a "sacrament of presence" pointing to the reality of God's gracious reign in the world, the Eucharist provides the basis for mission as transformation, reconciliation, and empowerment. It is also an effective sign that brings unity, one that transcends all human boundaries, be they racial, linguistic, national, gender, or social. The Eucharist brings God's eschatological reality into the life of the church, empowering it for mission and giving the world a foretaste of the coming consummation (1 Corinthians 11:26).

Mission is Spirit led: the Holy Spirit awakens, inspires, and guides Christ's followers to bear witness to Christ and to God's unconditional love. The Spirit revives and renews continuously the church for mission. Spiritual renewal is a gift of the visitation of the Holy Spirit. Church renewal may take the form of creative worship and liturgical, structural, missiological, and charismatic renewal, all of which are the working of the Holy Spirit using different gifts for different purposes. Although renewal can

> *As a "sacrament of presence" pointing to the reality of God's gracious reign in the world, the Eucharist provides the basis for mission as transformation, reconciliation, and empowerment.*

be imitated, its authenticity is attested to by its fruits in holistic mission.

Led by the Spirit and endowed with diverse gifts, the whole church is charismatic. "Charismatic" does not necessarily mean Pentecostal – the two terms are not interchangeable. A charismatic church uses all the gifts of the Spirit for mission: proclamation of the gospel, deliverance from evil powers, prayer for healing, community building, service, and advocacy. Charismatic renewal underscores the fact that the Christian faith concerns the whole human being: emotion, reason, will, and passion. This explains the fact that charismatic movements in churches account for the churches' rapid growth and expansion. Mission is experiential. It is necessary for the church, as the LWF Tenth Assembly urged, to find ways *to engage with Pentecostal churches and charismatic movements within our own churches.* Such engagement would enable the church to study, analyze, and learn from charismatic phenomena, with their positive and negative consequences – a learning that would prove beneficial for the church to serve more faithfully in God's mission.

> *Transformation is a continuous process of rejection of that which dehumanizes and desecrates life and adherence to that which affirms the sanctity of life and gifts in everyone and promotes peace and justice in society.*

2.3. Theological dimensions of mission

As the church participates in God's mission, empowered by the Word and led by the Spirit in the way of Christ, it engages faithfully and purposefully with the challenging contexts of the twenty-first century. Engaging prayerfully with the challenges of its context, the church, following the hermeneutical spiral, needs to deepen continuously its theological reflection on the different aspects and dimensions of mission. A continued theological reflection on the praxis of mission and on overarching missiological themes strengthens the church in carrying out its contextual mission.

2.3.1. Mission as Transformation, Reconciliation, and Empowerment

This document focuses on three dimensions of mission: **transformation**, **reconciliation**, and **empowerment**. These dimensions of mission are reflected in God's mission as creator, redeemer, and sanctifier and are enhanced in the missiological understanding of the threefold way of Christ: *the way of incarnation, the way of the cross, and the way of resurrection.* These mission dimensions permeate all mission endeavors (e.g., proclamation, service, advocacy for justice, interfaith dialogue, and care of creation) and provide criteria with which the church judges its faithfulness in mission before Christ, who has sent it into the world.

Transformation

The scriptures speak of transformation as an ongoing process of total reorientation of life with all its aspirations, ideologies, structures, and values. Transformation is a continuous process of rejection of that which dehumanizes and desecrates life and adherence to that which affirms the sanctity of life and gifts in everyone and promotes peace and justice in society. This comes from the knowledge of the gracious will of God, who calls, justifies, and empowers people, through the Holy Spirit, to be conformed to the image of God's Son, offering the self as the instrument of righteousness (Romans 12:2, 6:13, 8:29; 1 Peter 1:14–25; Ephesians 4:15–5:10; 2 Corinthians 3:18; Colossians 1:10–14; Titus 3:5).

Different sectors of society have worked energetically for change and progress, based on the insatiable human need for self-improvement and gain. Such a process of change, though laudable and at times useful, should not be confused with transformation, which from the perspective of the mission of the church is primarily God's work in the midst of creation. Transformation, perceived in the light of Christ's resurrection, is the unfolding of the potential life-giving nature of all creation and an expression of the working of God's grace in nature. It is the ongoing work of the Holy Spirit to effect transformation in and through the church to the whole world. Living with expectation in the "already and not yet" of God's redemption, the church must guard itself from a triumphalistic view of transformation and instead should accept it in faith with its ambiguities and uncertainties.

The church's mission as transformation encompasses individuals, structures, and relations in societies. For the individual, the apostle Paul, for instance, emphasizes that transformation is based fundamentally on God's saving grace, uniting the believer with Christ's death, burial, and resurrection, so that, like the resurrected Christ, she or he *"might walk in newness of life"* (Romans 6:4–14). Being justified by grace, the believing sinner, holding fast to God's promise that their life is hid with Christ in God (Colossians 3:3), responds in gratitude to the leading of the Spirit to walk in the way of Christ. Transformation as a gift of justification empowers people to denounce wickedness and to *"yield their*

members to God as instruments of righteousness" (Romans 6:13) and to endure the way of the cross, even death, for the healing of others (2 Corinthians 4:7–12). Such transformation explains what Paul says: *"And we all, with unveiled face, beholding the glory of the Lord, are being transformed into his likeness from one degree of glory to another; this comes from the Lord who is the Spirit"* (2 Corinthians 3:18).

© CAM Barbara Robra

© CAM Barbara Robra

The Holy Spirit also leads and empowers the church into a mission of transformation addressing structures and relations in society. Following Christ in the way of incarnation, the church enters deep into contexts, identifying itself fully with the plight of the victims of injustice, exploitation, and exclusion. With Christ in its midst, it stands in solidarity with those impoverished and dehumanized by neo-liberal economic globalization. It thus becomes the church of the poor. As it renounces and denounces unjust and violent practices and structures in public and domestic spheres as sinful and destructive to life in society, the church walks with Christ in the way of the cross. Mission as proclamation, service or diakonia, and advocacy must be carried out under the sign of the cross to strengthen solidarity and hope. Following Christ in the way of resurrection, the church, witnessing to the gospel through word, presence, and deed, does not let political and social oppression and economic exclusion have the last word. Through its mission as diakonia, which is not a mere token of faith, but purposefully aiming at sustainable community for all, the church is led by the Spirit to "make way out of no way."

As it walks in the way of Christ in the midst of a broken and violent world, the church itself undergoes deep and often painful transformation. Seen from the way of Christ, transformation is not always experienced as a glorious or joyous event. Liberation, as well as reconciliation, for instance, may require the painful experience of giving up power and privileges. As transformation necessitates "swimming against the tide" it may imply making sacrifices, enduring persecution, or even facing martyrdom.

Reconciliation

Scripture clearly states that one of the aims of God's mission is reconciliation: *"God was in Christ reconciling the world to himself ... and entrusting to us the message of reconciliation"* (2 Corinthians 5:19). The church in mission participates in God's reconciling mission as God's ambassador, beseeching people on behalf of Christ to be reconciled with God. This is a foundational aspect of reconciliation: restoring the relationship between God and human beings. By means of proclamation and witness through Christian living and diakonia, individuals are brought to repentance and faith and rejoice in being accepted into God's communion of the "sent." The grace of this unmerited and unhoped-for reconciliation makes it possible to extend reconciliation to all other human relations: within a family, with other groups, in society, and between nations. As an ambassador of reconciliation, a peacemaker, the church's mission tasks include mediation, restoration of peaceful coexistence, and the building and sustaining of relations. To assume this responsibility for reconciliation, the church takes its inspiration from Christ's threefold way. Walking the way of the cross, the church takes upon itself the pains of victims and the arrogance of perpetrators in order to make room for peace and reconciliation. To convince perpetrators to own up to their wrongdoing and commit to a restoration of justice is a very difficult task. However, God's reconciling power is made perfect through the vulnerability or foolishness of the mission of the church.

The church's mission of reconciliation extends also to the international sphere. In the twenty-first century many countries are still living with the legacy of previous centuries' oppression and injustice. Countries that struggled under colonialism are now suffering from a poverty-inducing neo-liberal economy driven by economic globalization. Such death-dealing structures and systems should not have the last word in a world where God has broken the finality of death. The mission of the church, in the way of resurrection, is to make liberation and reconciliation possible for both the oppressed and the oppressors. Liberation and reconciliation have to go together. Liberation without due consideration of eventual reconciliation is self-defeating; reconciliation without liberation is unrealistic and ideological. Reconciliation and liberation require the implementation of restorative justice at the national and international levels, to allow victims of oppression and injustice to regain their human dignity. Through this liberating reconciliation and reconciling liberation the church initiates a process of transformation, anticipating the final reconciliation of all things in God's eschatological reign.

Empowerment

Speaking of empowerment in mission reflects the words of Jesus: *"But you shall receive power when the Holy Spirit has come upon you; and you shall be my witnesses … to the end of the earth"* (Acts 1:8). Empowerment refers here primarily to God sharing power (*dynamis*) with people for participation in God's mission. God empowers individual Christians and the whole church through the leading of the Holy Spirit and the bestowing of spiritual gifts necessary to carry out the holistic mission of the church. Divine empowerment effects in people Jesus' promise that whoever believes in him will do the work that he does, and even greater work. The church is empowered to witness to God's unconditional love in Jesus Christ in a world where hatred abounds, to speak of justification by grace in a world where all seem to be measured by their market value, and to prophesy hope in the midst of untold violent suffering and despair.

This is a foundational aspect of reconciliation: restoring the relationship between God and human beings.

The Holy Spirit empowers the church to resist misusing power

as "power over" others and to walk in the way of Christ, where power is shared with all. In the church, every baptized believer is endowed with a special gift for mission, for mutual up-building and encouragement. Whether they be male or female, lay or clergy, young or old, all their gifts are to be developed, appreciated, and availed. The church is not a divide between the powerless and those with power capable of empowering others. Rather, as the church walks the way of Christ, it benefits from the mutual empowerment of its members, an empowerment flowing from the presence of the empowering Triune God in its midst.

God's empowerment extends also to society at large through the mission activities of the church as one of God's empowering instruments in the world. Through its service and diaconal ministries, the church provides help for the immediate needs of people in distress (e.g., refugees, displaced persons, victims of natural disasters). However, the church is called to go beyond a "hand out " or charity ministry to a mission of empowerment. The church seeks ways to assist those in need, regardless of their origin or creed, to regain their human dignity by asserting control over their own lives. For the missional church, "those in need" refers not only to the materially, economically, and socially deprived, but also to those with emotional, relational, mental, and spiritual needs. People who suffer from different manic-depressive syndromes, such as confused identity, low self-esteem, depression, and other psychosocial illnesses, require the attention and presence of the church in much the same way as the economically and socially marginalized and oppressed.

> *As the church walks the way of Christ, it benefits from the mutual empowerment of its members, an empowerment flowing from the presence of the empowering Triune God in its midst.*

2.3.2. Mission as holistic and contextual praxis

The church in mission understands its participation in God's mission as contextual, addressing faithfully the challenges of ever changing and complex contexts and, thus, comprehensive and holistic. Mission is holistic and contextual with regard to its aim, practice, and location. Its aim encompasses the whole of creation (ecological concerns), the whole of life (social, political, economic, and cultural), and the whole human being (i.e., all people and the whole person – spiritual, mental, relational, physical, and environmental needs). Its practice calls for the participation of the whole church, women and men, young and old. Being holistic, mission flows from the being of the church as worshipping, messenger, serving, healing, and oikumene community. As such a community, the church seeks justice through advocacy, effects transformation through empowerment, and works for peace and reconciliation. Given the catholicity of the church, mission happens in all places, wherever the church is, and in all times to all generations. Thus, every church is responsible for mission tasks in its locality, but should also be prepared to cooperate with others in different localities when called to partnership, and to engage in joint mission ventures in places where "no one has gone before."

As the church engages in mission praxis holistically and contextually, it is faced with dialectically interrelated missiological issues that require clarification. On various occasions and for a long time, mission departments and societies, mission institutes, and individual Christians have engaged in theological discussions and debates on the relation between mission praxes such as proclamation and service, justification and justice, salvation and healing, and mission and interfaith dialogue. Finding clarity on such issues will help greatly in the church's understanding and practice of holistic mission.

Proclamation and service

The church's holistic mission encompasses proclamation and service or diakonia. How are they related in the real praxis of mission? The gospel is primarily the good news of God's gracious justification of the sinner through faith in Jesus Christ. As a living, creative word of God, the gospel is to be verbalized and articulated in a language understandable to people in their contexts and time. Proclamation as evangelism focuses on making sure that the gospel is proclaimed to all people by the whole church and that the good news addresses specific contexts concretely and relevantly. Evangelism leads people to personal encounter with the living God, inviting them to respond positively in faith to Christ's gracious call to follow. The church invites people through the evangelistic proclamation to receive the gift of the forgiveness of sins in baptism, to join a fellowship of the Christian community, and to live a life of discipleship in mission.

Service, which is an integral part of mission, is an essential expression of diakonia. The letter from the LWF global consultation on *"Prophetic Diakonia: For the Healing of the World"* (2002) (cf. publication in 2003) highlights the fact that diakonia is a core component of the gospel itself, and is thus central to what it means to be the church. Diakonia is not merely an option but an essential part of discipleship. All Christians are called through baptism to live out diakonia through what they do and how they live in the world. It begins as unconditional service to the neighbor in need and leads inevitably to social change and transformation.

In Lutheran churches, diakonia is expressed in various forms: international relief and development work, diaconal institutions, advocacy for peace, justice, and integrity of creation, congregational diaconal work, and social ministries. When carrying out these ministries, the church is mindful of two

theological issues. First, diakonia is more than mere charity. The church understands diakonia to be interrelated deeply with *Kerygma* (proclamation) and *Koinonia* (sharing at the table) and thus as inevitably prophetic. It goes beyond initial reaction to immediate needs, tackling the root causes of poverty and debilitating structural and systemic violence. In prophetic diakonia the paternalistic dichotomy between "wealthy givers" and "poor

© CAM Barbara Robra

receivers" is overcome, for both the served and the serving are transformed together in their common endeavor to challenge injustice. Second, being rooted in the theology of the cross, the church is spiritually led to identify itself with the suffering and excluded. The purpose of its diaconal work is not to proselytize (to attract other Christians to one's own denomination). In emergencies especially, the church does not use people's vulnerability as an occasion to impose its Christian beliefs.

The church and individual Christians proclaim the gospel by word and bear witness to it by the way they live in every situation in their own contexts. There has to be a coherence of living and speaking, of word and deed. Proclaiming and witnessing through diakonia are inseparable as participation in God's transforming, reconciling, and empowering mission in the world. Word without deed can be abstract and powerless, and deed without word can be mute and open for any interpretation.

Service, which is an integral part of mission, is an essential expression of diakonia.

Of course, there may be times and places in the world where oral proclamation of the gospel would not be possible and the only way of witnessing is a wordless service rooted in prayer. This wordless service may have many faces, such as humanitarian assistance, diaconal work, and advocating for social and political transformation.

Justification and justice

God's justification of the sinner by grace transcends all human concepts and systems of justice based on the law of merits, retribution, distribution, reparation, and retaliation. Justification by grace does not focus on what the sinner has done or promises to do, but on what God offers. What God offers is an invitation, signed with the blood of Christ, to life in communion with God. It is God's gracious invitation that justifies humankind's being in this life and it is also God's unmerited invitation that justifies the faithful's belonging to God's household, that is the divine communion.

Justification by grace, therefore, is liberating and creative. It liberates human beings *from* constant preoccupation about self-justification, self-worth, and achievement and creates new beginnings and possibilities *for* life in abundance. God's liberating and creative justice is also at work in God's mighty acts in history, when the afflicted receive encouragement, the captives are released, and the oppressed are set free. This liberation initiates the rebirth of life in community where solidarity, reconciliation, and justice may blossom (Isaiah 61:1–7). The church's engagement in advocating for and working towards the establishment of justice flows from God's liberating and creative justice at work in God's mission, in which the missional church participates. As God's grace creates the space for liberating justice to unfold, the church is called to discern the form in which justice will take shape in society. The church needs to reflect prayerfully on the kind of justice that will bring transformation, reconciliation, and empowerment in and for society.

© LWF Margret Stasius

Justification by grace does not let injustice or any instrument of sin and wickedness go unchallenged. Faith in the God who justifies by grace inspires and energizes the church "to do justice, to love kindness and to walk humbly with God" (Micah 6:8).

Salvation and healing

God's mission in the world includes the experience of healing in the context of community life, as well as the spiritual reality of salvation through the redeeming presence of Christ in the life of the Christian community, both corporately and individually. Salvation as the eschatological promise that one day God will be all in all remains in constant tension with the harsh reality of life and its longing for healing. Healing encompasses questions pertaining to health and sickness, and medical, psychiatric, emotional, and spiritual treatment and cure. For Christians of all denominations, healing is a basic theological theme, as it plays a significant role in spiritual life. The existence of disease and the fact that not every sick person among Christians receives healing raise questions about the relation of healing to salvation in Jesus Christ.

According to the scriptures, God is the source of all healing. In the Old Testament, healing and salvation are interrelated and in many instances mean the same thing: "Heal me, O Lord, and I shall be healed; save me, and I shall be saved" (Jeremiah 17:14). The New Testament, however, does not equate being cured from an ailment with being saved. The New Testament also makes a distinction between curing and healing. Some may be cured but not healed (Luke 17:15–19), while others are not cured but healed (2 Corinthians 12:7–9). "Cure" denotes restoring lost health and thus carries

a protological view. Healing refers to the eschatological reality of abundant life that breaks in through the event of Jesus Christ, the wounded healer, who participates in all aspects of human suffering, dying, and living, and overcomes violation, suffering, and death by his resurrection. In this sense, healing and salvation point to the same eschatological reality.

Mission and interfaith dialogue

To differing degrees, churches have engaged in dialogue with people of diverse faiths and convictions. The relevance and aims of such dialogue in relation to the mission of the church has been a much-debated theme in theological discourse. Questions have been raised as to whether dialogue should replace mission outreach, or serve as a preliminary step for mission, or be an integral part of the comprehensive mission of the church.

Interfaith dialogue, as the search for peace and cooperation in society, for mutual understanding and for the truth, is an integral part of the mission of the church. As the church is called and sent to bring transformation, healing, and reconciliation in society,

working with different groups of people to achieve peace and cooperate for the establishment of justice pertains to its mission. Interreligious dialogue, for instance, is an effective instrument to defuse religious tensions and to identify ways for the multireligious community to tackle the problems of poverty, discrimination, violence, and development in general.

Conversely, Christianity, like Islam and other religions, is a missionary religion. Sharing its faith with others is basic to its identity. Jesus blessed and commanded his disciples to make disciples of all nations (Matthew 28:18–20). Christ offers salvation and healing to all humankind by faith alone, without human merits. This uniqueness of Christ is foundational to the church's mission. As the LWF Tenth Assembly stated in its message: *"God's mission is wider than the bounds of the church."* However, quoting from the WCC Mission and Evangelism Conference, San Antonio, 1996, it added: *"We cannot point to any other way to salvation than Jesus Christ; at the same time we cannot set limits to the saving power of God. Coming to a positive understanding of the nature of missionary religions, and how to accommodate their need to propagate, can be a major theme in interfaith dialogues. However, interfaith dialogue should not aim at converting or winning over dialogue partners"*.

Furthermore, theologians have focused on the Trinity as a theological model for interfaith dialogue. A Trinitarian model not only makes space and allows for the existence of the other, but also provides the theological basis and models for the practice of the "common search for truth" in interfaith dialogue. For the church, a Trinitarian approach may provide the possibility of underlining the uniqueness of Christ, while at the same time confessing to the Holy Spirit's influence outside the church and God's work in creation and in other religions.

Focusing on the inner relation and the interdependence of the Triune life of God provides a basis for a dialogue through life shared in community, as well as through the sharing together of a spiritual journey of the soul as people of faiths. The Trinitarian model also reveals a transformational aspect to interfaith dialogue. As the Son ventures into the unknown while trusting in the Father and with the accompaniment of the Spirit, the church also ventures into dialogue with people of diverse faiths, holding to the eschatological vision that in the end God will be all in all. Trusting in God's future empowers the church to engage in incarnational and transformational living together with people of diverse faiths as close companions on the Emmaus road. This does not diminish Christians' testimony that they have found life in abundance in Jesus Christ. It is only when they are willing to listen with open minds and hearts to what matters most to people of faith that their own witness can be heard in its integrity.

2.4. Theology, context, and practice

Mission as accompaniment needs a theology that is reflective of and developed in the context of the church. Such contextual mission theology must also reflect on the praxis of the church. Mission theology, using the hermeneutical spiral, already refers to and draws from the practice of mission.

> *Interreligious dialogue, for instance, is an effective instrument to defuse religious tensions and to identify ways for the multi-religious community to tackle the problems of poverty, discrimination, violence, and development in general.*

The aim of section three of this document is to look at the practice of mission as an indication of how the church in mission lives out its calling to participate in God's mission. Mission flows from its being as a witnessing, missional church. The purpose of the third section, therefore, is not to provide a prescription for mission practices for all situations, nor to enumerate the various mission tasks that the church must perform. Rather, it indicates general directions and impulses of mission practices that, it is hoped, will initiate creative discussions and inspire imaginative programs and projects among churches and their related agencies.

PRACTICE OF MISSION

So they drew near to the village to which they were going. He appeared to be going further, but they constrained him, saying, "Stay with us, for it is toward evening and the day is now far spent." So he went in to stay with them. When he was at table with them, he took the bread and blessed, and broke it, and gave it to them. And their eyes were opened and they recognized him; and he vanished out of their sight. They said to each other, "Did not our hearts burn within us while he talked to us on the road, while he opened to us the scriptures?" And they rose that same hour and returned to Jerusalem; and they found the eleven gathered together and those who were with them, who said, "The Lord has risen indeed, and has appeared to Simon!" Then they told what had happened on the road, and how he was known to them in the breaking of the bread. Luke 24:28–35

SECTION 3

PRACTICE OF MISSION

3.1. The whole church in mission

The church understands mission as a faithful expression of its calling, namely to point to and participate in God's in-breaking reign in Christ Jesus. The mission of the church, in its different forms and aspects, aims at transformation, reconciliation, and empowerment in and of the world. Mission is God's gift to every baptized person, as well as to the whole church: from the congregation, to the national church, to the worldwide communion of churches. The whole church (i.e., every member) participates in mission, for mission is not the prerogative of a few professionals or a few wealthy congregations and churches. Mission by proxy is a foreign concept in the mission of God, meaning that the church cannot outsource its missionary role any more than it can outsource its worship and sacramental life. Mission is also the calling of the whole church, not only individuals, and thus is the responsibility of the whole household of God, the communion of the sent.

Engaging in mission from the perspective of the communion of the sent (and also of the saints) leads the church to faithful *martyria* as it stands together in all places at all times in common witness. As the church practices mission as a communion, and not only as isolated individual congregations or churches, solidarity and partnership in mission will develop and competition and wasteful duplications will cease. Lutheran churches, for instance, when participating in God's mission as a communion of Lutheran churches, will reap the blessings of shared mission resources. The mission endeavor itself will benefit from the wealth of experience gleaned from around the world and from different generations of Christians.

Since mission must be contextual for the faith to be rooted in people's real life experience, every church assumes primary responsibility for mission in its immediate locality and region. However, because of the apostolicity and catholicity of the church, proximity does not mean exclusive ownership of the practice of mission. Mission remains God's mission; thus, individual Christians or families from different parts of the world may receive a call, from God through a sister church, to share mission responsibility with another church in a different geographical location or sociocultural situation. From this perspective, the role of and training for specialized ministries for international partnership in mission are very important. Care must be taken, however, that calling cross-cultural witnesses as missionaries, co-workers, or advisers does not divide the communion into "sender" and "receiver" churches.

Given the increasing complexity of today's contexts of mission, partnership in mission is more crucial than ever before. New models of partnership that promote equal participation and sharing of responsibility are being tried. Churches in the North and the South are now talking about *accompaniment* in mission. As the word accompaniment comes from companion, which means "sharing bread together," companion churches in mission share all their resources with one another. As in the Emmaus story, companions share the journey together with all the concerns, pains, hopes, and joys that each one brings. The resurrected Christ, who joins the journey, makes the companionship empowering and transforming for the church and the world.

In some churches, for historical and structural reasons, mission is still carried out through independent, church-related agencies. This practice needs further and deeper theological reflection in light of the ecclesiological understanding of the church as missional. In order to avoid blurring the roles and responsibilities of the church itself in God's mission, some mission agencies have taken the initiative to challenge the church to reflect on the nature of the church as missional. Integrating mission into church structures, locally and globally, as well as bringing together witnessing through word and deed into one structure, would be part of the discussion.

> *Word empowered and Spirit led, the church knows that mission flows from its nature as a witnessing community.*

3.2. The missional church in action

For the missional church, mission is not only what the church does (missionary activities), but also the church at work. Word empowered and Spirit led, the church knows that mission flows from its nature as a witnessing community. The ministry of the church in its various forms plays a central role in equipping the church for mission as a worshipping, messenger, serving, healing, and oikumene community.

3.2.1. A witnessing community

The church, as a witnessing community, points to the in-breaking of God's reign in Christ in the world, using all the spiritual gifts (*charismata*) that the Holy Spirit has generously bestowed upon it. According to 1 Corinthians 12, the church is endowed with spiritual gifts for the strengthening of the communion/fellowship (*Koinonia*), for the proclamation of the gospel (*Kerygma*), and for service and healing (*Diakonia*). As a witnessing community, the church cannot participate faithfully in God's mission without these gifts, lest mission become a mere human enterprise. A church in mission is a gifted (*charismatic*) church for a transforming, reconciling, and empowering mission.

A worshipping community

As a worshipping community the church points to the reality and presence of God's gracious reign in Christ, which calls together and sustains, through Word and Sacraments, a faithful community of forgiven sinners. In and of itself, a praying, confessing, and celebrating community is a sign of God's in-breaking reign.

> *As a worshipping community the church points to the reality and presence of God's gracious reign in Christ, which calls together and sustains, through Word and Sacraments, a faithful community of forgiven sinners.*

The worshipping community also points to the future with God, an eschatological reality that is coming towards the present. Thus, the church prays for and expects that God's new reality will break forth in its worship. Because of what it is and what it expects, the church is empowered through worship for transforming and reconciling mission in the world. Serious planning and preparation for worship services in view of the mission of the church, keeping in mind the spiritual importance of welcoming hospitality, are therefore crucial.

A nurturing community

As a nurturing community, the church sees itself as a learning community and learning in community. The nurturing or discipling of God's people for mission is an important dimension of the mission of the church. Equipping the whole church for mission (Ephesians 4:11–12) includes Christian education and theological education. Christian education provides accompaniment for a lifelong journey of faith. Some churches understand Christian education missiologically as "going deep in order to go wide" and as "teach to reach." Theological education is fundamental for ensuring the continuity of holistic and prophetic ministries that strengthen the church's mission of reconciliation and empowerment. Recent missiological awakening among theological seminaries and Bible schools has caused a shift in curriculum – mission no longer considered as an elective course but as an integral part of all core courses. This shift by no means undermines the role of mission departments or institutes in universities and seminaries. On the contrary, it seeks to enhance their importance as being central to the nurturing ministry of the church.

For the worshipping and nurturing community, prayer is at the center of all that it does. Prayer is the medium through which the church places its trust in the "calling, sending, and accompanying" God, a trust constantly renewed and strengthened by an ever deepened sense of mission spirituality. Prayer, however, is also the medium through which God brings transformation, reconciliation, empowerment, and healing into the world (Matthew 21:22; John 14:12–14, 15:16). A church in mission, indwelled and led by the Holy Spirit, is a praying church.

A messenger community

The church in mission is a messenger community. It has a powerful and empowering message to deliver. The message is centered on God's reconciliation and salvation in Jesus Christ and thus also points to God's gracious act of transformation of the whole person and of all people in all places at all times. The church in mission is apostolic, not only because it delivers the message entrusted to it, but also because it is faithful to the integrity of the message. While announcing the in-breaking of God's reign, the message is also prophetically denouncing oppressive, hierarchical, and patriarchal structures and destructively violent systems, as well as sinful interpersonal relations. Announcing the message prophetically compels the messenger community to analyze and name its context ever anew.

© LWF Margret Stasius

The messenger community understands that the message of the breaking in of God's gracious reign in Christ can be conveyed in different ways: in verbal proclamation, by living the call to be a good neighbor, and through diaconal services and advocacy for justice and peace. In the past, many churches had a rather restricted definition of mission as basically evangelism, an encounter between unbelief and faith. While proclamation as evangelism is at the core of mission, it is not the whole of mission. Since the 1970s, churches, especially from the South, have understood mission in a more holistic and comprehensive way. The messenger community bears witness to the Good News in word and deed, making the life promised by the gospel concrete in the experience of people in their own contexts, affording opportunities for the wider community to share in God's gracious invitation to the "wedding feast" (Matthew 22:1–12).

The messenger community knows of different ways of inviting people to be part of the in-breaking reign of God. Churches thus far have embarked on evangelistic "campaigns" in stadia, tents, street corners, or moving from village to village and from door to door. Progress has been made in the use of modern technology such as radio, audio and video cassettes, and television. Many churches nowadays are exploring effective use of the Internet or the telephone for sharing God's message. These communication tools, though they may be effective in reaching large secularized audiences, are rather impersonal. "Virtual" congregations are created through the Internet, but people continue to long for a real faith community. The church is therefore challenged to reconsider traditional forms and means of communication.

One approach that is still effective is the personal, one on one, face-to-face, cross-generational and cross-cultural way of sharing the Good News. This approach is open, flexible, and affordable to all messengers. It can be practiced everywhere – at home, at work or study places, while traveling. Looking at its context as a messenger community, however, the church realizes that Christians in some affluent and secularized countries are hesitant or even reluctant to share their faith openly with others. The church needs to undertake an in-depth study of its context, theology, and ministry to find the causes of Christians' inability to live fully as messengers.

> *One approach that is still effective is the personal, one on one, face-to-face, cross-generational and cross-cultural way of sharing the Good News.*

In some parts of the world, where the "one on one" sharing of holistic mission has been practiced, usually through the "house church movement" and renewal charismatic movements, church membership has grown tremendously. In Africa, for instance, the Lutheran church grows on average by 300,000 members every year. The church is faced with the great need of providing adequate pastoral care, nurturing, and structural capacity. However, the messenger community, through these movements, has found an effective way of being the church in community seven days a week.

A serving community

The church in mission is a serving community engaged in diakonia in the image of its Lord, who said that he came *"not to be served but to serve, and to give his life as a ransom for many"* (Matthew 20:28). Through diakonia, the church as a serving community expresses concretely in people's everyday lives the in-breaking reign of God in Christ. On the one hand, churches have been engaged in diaconal work, such as schools, hospitals, orphanages, and nursing homes. In spite of the benefits that society at large has gained from such services, they have been criticized by some as "evangelistic"; that is, done with the aim of alluring or attracting people for the sole purpose of "winning souls". The church, through its services, bears witness to the reality of God's in-breaking reign in Christ, whether the service is for the community at large or for the church's own nurturing. However, it realizes that such service may become paternalistic and proselytizing, and should be the object of continuous reflection and discernment.

On the other hand, the serving community is also known for its engagement in diakonia with social services aimed primarily at relieving human and

© LWF

community needs, effecting transformational processes in structures and in the lives of communities. The primary aim is to share with all people, in concrete ways, the abundant life promised by the gospel, without necessarily "vocalizing" or verbalizing it in any way. Such services are not mere charity. They aim at transforming communities and societies, advocating for justice, and calling for alternative sustainable communities; thus, they must be results oriented and impact conscious. This unconditional and non-discriminatory diaconal service takes shape usually through the church's development projects: emergency work, humanitarian aid, rehabilitation work after a catastrophe, community development work, and different care activities.

The concept of development is considered by its detractors as incompatible with the mission of the church, as denoting a Western political economic theory based on a specific understanding of social relations and using modernist views. The understanding of the meaning and aim of development, however, has changed drastically. Development has been refocused to aim at the emancipation of the individual and the transformation and liberation of society, encompassing the social, cultural, and spiritual well-being of people. It is no longer focused solely on economic and material wealth. In this understanding, development work, as part of the

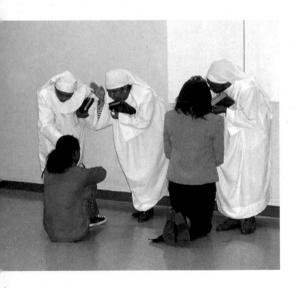

All photos © LWF

process of transformation and empowerment, is an integral part of the mission of the church. In many parts of the world, at the grassroots level, the church as a serving community is recognized as an effective agent of in-depth social empowerment and transformation.

A healing community

The church in mission is a healing community. From the very beginning, the church has understood its calling and sending to be a healing community as an integral part of its service in community (Matthew 10:1, 8; Mark 16:15–18), following in the way of its Lord (Acts 4:30). It also understands itself as a community in the process of healing. Healing takes place at personal *and* societal levels. The church in mission has been endowed with various spiritual gifts for the healing of persons. Persons are cared for and receive treatment in church medical institutions for physical, mental, and even relational ailments. Hospitals, clinics, and emergency medical help are means through which the church has shown the mission of love and empowerment. One of the challenging tasks of the church in the present day is to address the complex issue of HIV/AIDS. Facing the challenge of the pandemic together with different churches, Lutheran

churches in the North and South engaged actively in the LWF campaign against HIV/AIDS (cf. *LWF Plan of Action: Conversion, Compassion, and Care*, 2002).

The church also continues the apostolic practice of healing through prayer and laying on of hands. Through this ministry, cure and healing, well-being and wholeness are prayed for, but the emphasis is on wholeness. Thus, the whole person, together with her or his relationships, is addressed, cared for, and transformed.

The church also looks at the problems and illnesses of society. As a nurturing, messenger, and serving community, the church works towards healing the deep wounds and lasting hurts caused by greed for power and materials, prejudice and violence in the world. At the start of the twenty-first century, many countries still bear the scars, shame, and resentment of colonialism, ideological conflict, racism, and genocide. Atrocities have been committed and suffered, humiliation imposed and endured, resources (material and human) plundered and lost. People – including former victims and victimizers – who share in the same healing community, wish to be relieved of such painful memories. Healing of memories, removing internalized guilt and the shame of the past, and finding paths together between countries, people, and churches should be a major challenge for church mission in this decade.

3.2.2. An *oikumene* community

The church in mission is an *oikumene* community. As it participates in God's mission, the church cares for the world as its *oikos*, house or home. It is also characteristic of the church in mission that though not *of* this world, it is *in* and *with* the world (John 17:15–18). The mission engagement of the church covers three aspects of the *oikos*: ecumenical, economic, and ecological. An expanded understanding and usage of the ecumenical household comes in also as dialogical engagement: fruitful dialogue with all people who call the earth their home.

Ecumenical engagement

Any church engaged in holistic mission in today's globalized contexts soon realizes that mission encompasses the "whole inhabited world" – not only selected areas – and is best carried out ecumenically by the whole household of God, beyond denominational demarcations. The inability of churches to achieve unity in diversity or to engage in joint mission ventures has undermined the credibility of the church in mission. Likewise, the many conflicts and dissensions among churches and between church-related organizations affect negatively the life and witness of the church. Energy, time, and resources are spent in trying to mediate and reconcile dissenting factions, rather than being focused on the well-being of the world.

A missional church as an *oikumene* community puts priority on bringing peace, justice, health, and abundant life to the *oikos*. Inspired by the spirit of reconciliation, it engages prophetically with the increasing political and social instability and violence in different places in the world. Both at the national and international levels, churches have courageously offered mediation between conflicting and warring parties. On many occasions, they have called even the most belligerent to the negotiation table in order to reach peaceful settlements between factions. Thus, for the healing of the world, it is imperative that understanding, solidarity, patience, and love are established among the churches. While church unity is one of the aims of mission, ecumenical dialogues between Christian denominations need to have mission at their center.

> *Healing of memories, removing internalized guilt and the shame of the past, and finding paths together between countries, people, and churches should be a major challenge for church mission in this decade.*

A dialogical engagement

The church as an *oikumene* community gives great consideration to people of other religions and convictions that also call this world their home. The church's sustained engagement in transformation, reconciliation, and empowerment also finds expression in its different interrelated approaches in interfaith dialogue with people living in multi-religious contexts.

In Malaysia, for instance, Christians and Muslims engage in a "dialogue of life." In the daily life of the community, people accept each other as people of faith and live together and interact with each other in peace. In 2002 and 2004, the LWF organized a "Peace Summit" for Africa, bringing together all religious leaders. The Summit established a Plan of Action aimed at jointly working for peace throughout the continent.

In India, there is a move to look for common ground that brings people of different faith traditions together for *dia-praxis*: action together in solidarity that engages in the promotion of justice, a better quality of life, and the alleviation of human suffering.

In other places, like Nigeria, and in multicultural cities in the North, Christians and Muslims engage in dialogue seeking understanding. Understanding of the other side's religious belief helps build mutual respect and trust, which facilitate cooperation for peace and development in society. Equally important is the "spiritual approach" in interfaith dialogue, practiced in India, emphasizing prayer and meditation. These approaches highlight a way of life that respects the image of God in everyone. Life is the medium of dialogue.

Another approach consists of academic interfaith dialogue. For

> *Transformation, reconciliation, and empowerment can and do take place in society through the church's encounter and dialogue with groups engaged in social, economic, and ecological concerns.*

the most part, this involves scholars and religious leaders. At this level, partners in dialogue need to be open, in all objectivity and honesty, to the truth claim presented by the other, and with the clear possibility of changing sides if what is presented shakes the foundation of their faith. For the church, this common search for truth is a trustful venture into the unknown, following the Trinitarian model of dialogue (cf. the LWF publication *Dialogue and Beyond*, March 2003).

Moreover, the church is constantly called to dialogue with different non-governmental organizations (NGOs) and civil societies on important issues contributing to the well-being of people and relations in society. Transformation, reconciliation, and empowerment can and do take place in society through the church's encounter and dialogue with groups engaged in social, economic, and ecological concerns.

Economic engagement

Christians live out their baptismal vocation in various arenas of daily life, including economic life. Here, people seek to pursue livelihoods, for their own families as well as for the wider community. A problem is that patterns of injustice, especially as they have emerged under economic globalization, make that increasingly difficult for many. Thus, it is important that the church as an *oikumene* community raise its prophetic voice against oppressive and unjust structures and systems, while also encouraging its members who have access to these structures to change policies and practices from within.

Churches locally, regionally, and globally have strategized together to advocate for the establishment of justice and peace and the eradication of poverty and killer diseases. The *oikumene* community is engaged in mission in a world which can destroy itself many times over and that seems unable or unwilling to eradicate poverty and hunger for all. Thus, the church prays for God's empowerment and guidance. It also searches for ways to empower the victims of injustice and engages proactively in transforming the adverse effects of neo-liberal economic globalization.

One example of joint action is the call for a "globalization of solidarity." This aims at fostering and promoting common strategies for debt cancellation for impoverished countries, protecting vulnerable economies from powerful transnational corporations, and supporting alternative trade agreements. Key to these and other strategies is the nurturing of a "spirituality of resistance" as an accompaniment to global solidarity. Churches can draw on their spiritual heritage to confront what is occurring under prevailing policies and practices, to equip members through congregational life to resist the operating assumptions, and work to transform the policies operating under economic globalization, in ecumenical, interfaith, and civil society partnerships. The Emmaus road story provides a powerful paradigm for the journey of churches as they engage with these challenges (cf. the LWF publication *A Call to Participate in Transforming Economic Globalization,* 2002, and the book, *Communion, Responsibility, Accountability,* 2004).

Ecological engagement

The *oikumene* community believes strongly in the goodness of God's creation. It is first and foremost *God's* creation, which is then received with gratitude as an *oikos* (home) for all people. The first step in the church's ecological mission engagement is that of confession and repentance. For centuries, the church's otherworldly outlook and its emphasis on human dominion or domination over creation paved the way for the exploitation and destruction of nature. The *oikos* earth is in agony.

© CAM Barbara Robra

The church as a healing community, in every place, needs to look at the whole of creation in the light of the gospel and search for ways to restore this planet to health. The world is not primarily a human environment, nor simply the stage for the drama of human salvation. Rather, it is in and of its own an active participant in God's mission. In the apostle Paul's vision, *"creation itself will be set free from its bondage to decay and obtain the glorious liberty of the children of God"* (Romans 8:20–21). The church as oikumene community, with its worldwide networks, should further and prioritize its participation in the process of rehabilitating the earth and preventing further ecological destruction caused by the use of fossil fuels, toxic waste pollution, and the extermination of species, for example. Together with civil societies and voluntary groups concerned about the integrity of the earth, there is an urgent need for the church to raise its prophetic voice in naming and denouncing destructive actions against the *oikos*. Local projects dealing with ecological rehabilitation should be encouraged and supported financially by all partners. Ecological engagement is an urgent mission call for all.

© Henri Fallon, http://henrisson.net

3.3. New challenges and opportunities for mission

The section on the *context of mission* describes in vivid terms the challenges and opportunities that the changing contexts of mission present. As the pace of globalization rapidly increases with the help of high technology, the market mentality and its attendant consumerism has already infected all spheres of life. It is tragic that the very things that promote globalization (e.g., wealth, information technologies, and skill) are precisely those which divide the world by excluding the majority. Moreover, it is ironic that in a world of high technology and abundant information and knowledge, violence has reached an unprecedented intensity and ubiquity. Contexts have changed radically, and as mission should always be contextual, there is a need for the church to scrutinize, inventory, and reshape its mission practices, with the aim of making them relevant and effective in and for today's contexts.

3.3.1. Mission to the "end of the earth"

Jesus promised his disciples that they would be empowered by the Holy Spirit to be his witnesses even "to the end of the earth" (Acts 1:8). The gospel has since been preached to all six continents, but there are still some places where the good news of God's grace in Christ has not been heard and received. In North and South, two thirds of the world's population do not yet or no longer recognize Christ as Lord and Savior.

With the shifting of Christianity's center of gravity from the North to the South, the majority of people in what were known as Christian countries have become indifferent or even hostile to the church's witness to the gospel. In countries such as these, there are spheres of life where Jesus Christ is no longer known. For the missional church, these "unreached" places or people are always considered the "end of the earth." These may not be far geographically, but may represent new situations, which offer new and challenging opportunities to witness (*martyria*) to the Lord of history.

Since the second half of the twentieth century, with its rapid changes in technology and the growth of entertainment industries, the church has been removed (in the real and metaphorical sense of the term) from the center of big cities. At the fringes of urban life and business, the church has had no significant influence on the life and future of urban communities. In the best of situations, the church has confined its mission to the care of individuals exasperated by urban demands. What new opportunities for mission do vast cosmopolitan cities such as São Paulo, New York, London, New Delhi, and Nairobi offer to the church? How can the church regain a meaningful presence and assert a relevant influence on the life of the city?

The point is not for the church to be in competition with politics, economics, and entertainment businesses for influence on the life of a city or a nation. Among the challenging opportunities for the church is to accompany communities and nations in "end of the earth" areas and situations and to dare to be the church "where no one has gone before." These are not necessarily "places," but may be spheres of life or interest groups or ideologies. For example, one of the common denominators in influencing and changing people's lives today is high technology. High tech, when rightly used, affords comfort and helps save lives, but in some cases artificial intelligence may rob people of their human dignity. Research into advanced information technology, genetic manipulation, and safe reusable energy sources is already underway. What would it take for the missional church to be at the birthing place of technology in order to make it more humane? Formulating ethical responses to the use of technology is necessary for the church, but it is not sufficient. The mission of the church calls for more proactive accompaniment.

There are opportunities for the church in accompanying people as they face the onslaught of thriving, destructive underground businesses that are pervasive, privatized, and hard to contain.

There are opportunities for the church in accompanying people as they face the onslaught of thriving, destructive underground businesses (e.g., the trafficking of drugs, arms, and women and children, and pornography through the Internet) that are pervasive, privatized, and hard to contain. More elusive is the exploitation in professional sports, spiritism, and secret cultic societies (which have a significant influence on international politics). The church in every locality/nation is best placed to identify those "end of the earth" areas and to design appropriate mission accompaniments.

3.3.2. Mission and the challenge of information technology

The rapid developments in communication and information technologies also influence mission contexts. There is a need for the church to reflect on the challenging opportunities that such changes bring to people's lives and to its mission in particular. Information technology (IT), for example, has revolutionized the way people communicate with each other, and also the way they think and live and, eventually, their way of being. The church in mission needs to find a new way of being church.

Many churches around the world are already using the Internet creatively for mission (e.g., the "virtual" or cyberspace church as a way to reach unchurched people; online worship services for Internet surfers). The challenge facing the church, however, is monumental. The Internet and a whole panoply of electronic gadgets (video games, DVDs, CDs, etc.) are often misused to promote a culture of violence. They affect deeply the way users live and think because of the dependency they create, especially among youth. Moreover, the church has to take seriously the challenge Internet culture presents to the way theology, theological education, and the nurturing of the baptized for discipleship and mission are done. This constitutes an "end of the earth" situation. As theology was once challenged in the North to measure up to philosophical presuppositions and norms, it is now challenged to keep pace with science and technology.

The challenge is not only to make theology survive the Internet culture's constant filtering of data in search of new, updated, and marketable information, but also for IT to be a useful tool for sharing the "old" but empowering story of Jesus Christ.

Since mission is contextual and is carried out by every church in every place, local congregations play a crucial role, especially in developing resources for mission.

The rapid development of IT has increased the gap between the haves and the have-nots: many people in the South are still waiting for their first telephone call or access to a computer. The church needs to address this situation urgently as part of its mission strategies.

3.3.3. Mission resources

The call to mission is good news to the church, hence the church must plan for it carefully. Stewardship of resources for the mission of the church is an important element in mission planning. At all church levels, starting with the congregation, allocation of resources for mission – human, material, and financial – should have high priority. Since mission is contextual and is carried out by every church in every place, local congregations play a crucial role, especially in developing resources for mission. A strong stewardship program at the congregational level, aiming at mission resources development, is the basis for reversing the dependency syndrome that has paralyzed many churches in debt-ridden countries. The contextual nature of mission calls on every congregation and national church to design mission activities purposefully based on available resources (e.g., human, material), while working for ways to increase access to other

© LWF

resources (e.g., technological, financial). A contextualized mission endeavor, with a strong sense of stewardship, avoids imported approaches that incur high overheads.

Moreover, as the church develops its stewardship program for mission resources, it needs to take a hard look at church structures to determine whether or not they facilitate the mission of the church. Church structures should be flexible and appropriate to the contexts and resource realities of each church and not

duplicates of foreign structures. Rigid and top-heavy church structures stifle the life and mission of the church in such a way that mission is reduced to only supporting church structures. Many churches in the South still depend on overseas subsidies, mainly for structural support.

The practice of mission as a communion of churches calls on churches to be dependent on each other in terms of mission resources: spiritual, human, material, and financial. Mission resources are primarily God's gifts, thus all churches are receivers and stewards of these gifts. On the one hand, therefore, interdependency in mission is for mutual empowerment and transformation based on mutual trust and accountability. The aim of this interdependency is not to ensure the well-being of the churches, but to strengthen their capacity for and competence in carrying out their mission. On the other hand, many churches in the South are faced with overwhelming challenges for mission (economic disaster, war, displaced population, famine, etc.) that stretch beyond local and national means. Churches in wealthier countries and their related agencies and mission departments, as stewards of God's gifts of mission resources, should reflect seriously and prayerfully on the question of "bilateralism" and "multilateralism" upholding interdependency in a multilateral way as an urgent mission challenge. Engaged in a mission of transformation, reconciliation, and empowerment, these churches and their related agencies, when dealing with project applications from poor countries and churches, should challenge and expose the predatory thinking, consumerist language, and dehumanizing ways of the market economy. They should help build a communion in mission that would be an alternative community, a haven of hope, empowering and supporting the victims of the adverse effects of globalization in all its expressions.

3.3.4. Mission pilgrimage

Recently, the practice of pilgrimage and retreat has received much interest among churches in Europe. Thousands of people, young and old, women and men, have taken time out of their busy schedules to commit themselves to a weekend or a week of spiritual experience of prayer, scriptural reading, singing, and silence (listening). In the past, individuals or small groups of individuals made pilgrimages for their own spiritual needs, and mission was not the primary aim. Nevertheless, churches and people encountered on the way were also spiritually uplifted.

A revival of pilgrimage as a mission practice could be extremely beneficial for today's churches. It could serve as a practical way for pilgrims to learn, experience, and form solidarity. Thus it could be an effective means of nurturing and promoting a "spirituality of resistance" as the church faces the onslaught of materialism, secularism, and consumerism. It could also present a great opportunity for mutual spiritual strengthening and witnessing in word and deed. Mission pilgrimage can be organized at local, national, regional, and global levels, as well as across generational and denominational lines.

The mission pilgrimage concept and practice help highlight a fundamental vision of the church as being in transformation, a nomadic church, a church on the way, on the Emmaus road. The church in mission is a church in pilgrimage. The church moves not only from place to place, but also from the present to the future and from this "age" to God's new aeon. As a nomadic, pilgrim church, it is gifted by the Holy Spirit to discern the signs of the time and to prophesy (point to) the breaking in of God's reign.

CONCLUSION

CONCLUSION

The understanding of the mission of the church has undergone significant paradigm shifts in the experience and praxes of the member churches of the Lutheran World Federation. For the Fourth Assembly (Helsinki, 1963), mission was still defined in a narrow sense as aiming at conversion from unbelief to faith. From the Sixth Assembly (Dar es Salaam, 1977) onward, however, mission was understood and practiced in a holistic way as encompassing proclamation, advocacy, and service to the whole person and to all people. More and more, advocacy for justice, peace, and integrity of creation was emphasized. At the LWF Global Consultation on Mission (Nairobi, 1998) transformation was considered an important dimension of mission, while joint ecumenical mission venture was seen as an important

aspect of mission practice in the twenty-first century. Continuing in the same vein, this document highlights the vision of the *missional church*, for which mission belongs to its very being as the body of Christ. It also highlights the understanding of mission as participating in the in-breaking of God's reign in Christ, sharing in a common journey with people in their contexts, and focusing on transformation, reconciliation, and empowerment.

These mission foci – transformation, reconciliation, and empowerment – aptly describe mission as the church's participation in the mission of the Triune God, Creator, Redeemer, and Sanctifier. They also reflect the characteristics of mission as holistic and contextual; namely, a mission led by the Holy Spirit to walk in the "way of the Son," the way of incarnation, cross, and resurrection. Mission is the *raison d'être* of the church. It flows from the nature of the church as a witnessing community, a gift of God's gracious justification for and invitation to mission.

One purpose of this document is to serve as a tool to accompany Lutheran churches in their self-analysis and reaffirmation of mission in their respective contexts. For this document to be such a tool, the churches are called to animate the hermeneutical spiral in real mission praxis. In order to reaffirm their mission meaningfully, the churches need to undertake serious analysis of their mission contexts, practices, and theology.

The context needs constant scrutiny and naming. The church at every level is called to discern the needs for transformation, reconciliation, and empowerment. In conducting such analysis, the church will be called to stand with the victims of injustice and violence and thus expose and denounce evil powers and situations that distort and disrupt creation and dehumanize life in society.

The church needs to take a critical look at how mission is practiced. Is mission a real praxis of faith intentionally aimed at effecting transformation, reconciliation, and empowerment in society, or is it simply practice? In light of this document, the church can examine how holistic and contextual its mission practices are. In fact, the church can conduct a mission practice assessment to determine, for instance, whether the whole church is engaged in the whole mission, or whether the different elements of mission (e.g., proclamation, service, advocacy, and care of creation) bring forth transformation, reconciliation, and empowerment. Whether resources are provided locally for the mission of the church can also be assessed. The church can thus identify new opportunities for mission and the resources and partnerships needed to address them effectively.

Finally, this document calls on the church to reaffirm its mission by reflecting ever anew on its mission theology. Theology should empower the church for mission, a mission that points to the reality of and participates in the in-breaking reign of God in Christ. Using the Emmaus road model of mission as being on a journey together, as accompaniment, this document invites Lutheran churches and other churches to engage in a theology that reflects on and draws from their contextual mission experience.

Using the Emmaus road model of mission as being on a journey together, as accompaniment, this document invites Lutheran churches and other churches to engage in a theology that reflects on and draws from their contextual mission experience.

Only such a theology can empower churches to unfold their holistic mission as accompaniment to people in every place, in their ever-changing contexts – a transforming, reconciling, and empowering mission.

"You shall receive power when the Holy Spirit has come upon you; and you shall be my witnesses in Jerusalem and in all Judea and Samaria and to the end of the earth." Acts 1:8